LESSONS OF THE HOLOCAUST

Although difficult to imagine, sixty years ago the Holocaust had practically no visibility in examinations of the Second World War. Yet today it is understood to be not only one of the defining moments of the twentieth century but also a touchstone in a quest for directions on how to avoid such catastrophes.

In *Lessons of the Holocaust*, Michael R. Marrus challenges the notion that there are definitive lessons to be deduced from the destruction of European Jewry. Instead, drawing on decades of studying, writing about, and teaching the Holocaust, he shows how its "lessons" are constantly challenged, debated, altered, and reinterpreted.

A succinct, stimulating analysis by a world-renowned historian, *Lessons of the Holocaust* is the perfect guide for the general reader to the historical and moral controversies that infuse the interpretation of the Holocaust and its significance.

(UTP Insights)

MICHAEL R. MARRUS is the Chancellor Rose and Ray Wolfe Professor Emeritus of Holocaust Studies at the University of Toronto. He is the author or co-author of eight books, including the award-winning *The Holocaust in History*.

UTP Insights

UTP Insights is an innovative collection of brief books offering accessible introductions to the ideas that shape our world. Each volume in the series focuses on a contemporary issue, offering a fresh perspective anchored in scholarship. Spanning a broad range of disciplines in the social sciences and humanities, the books in the UTP Insights series contribute to public discourse and debate and provide a valuable resource for instructors and students.

BOOKS IN THE SERIES

- Michael R. Marrus, *Lessons of the Holocaust*
- William Watson, *The Inequality Trap: Fighting Capitalism Instead of Poverty*
- Phil Ryan, *After the New Atheist Debate*
- Paul Evans, *Engaging China: Myth, Aspiration, and Strategy in Canadian Policy from Trudeau to Harper*

Also by Michael R. Marrus

The Politics of Assimilation: French Jews at the Time of the Dreyfus Affair
Vichy France and the Jews (with Robert O. Paxton)
The Unwanted: European Refugees in the Twentieth Century
The Holocaust in History
Mr. Sam: The Life and Times of Samuel Bronfman
The Nuremberg War Crimes Trial, 1945–46: A Documentary History
Some Measure of Justice: The Holocaust-Era Restitution Campaign of the 1990s

LESSONS OF THE HOLOCAUST

Michael R. Marrus

UNIVERSITY OF TORONTO PRESS
Toronto Buffalo London

© University of Toronto Press 2016
Toronto Buffalo London
www.utppublishing.com
Printed in the U.S.A.

ISBN 978-1-4426-3005-5 (cloth)
ISBN 978-1-4426-3006-2 (paper)

Printed on acid-free, 100% post-consumer recycled paper

Library and Archives Canada Cataloguing in Publication

Marrus, Michael R., 1941–, author
Lessons of the Holocaust/Michael R. Marrus.

Includes bibliographical references and index.
ISBN 978-1-4426-3005-5 (cloth)   ISBN 978-1-4426-3006-2 (paper)

1. Holocaust, Jewish (1939–1945) – Historiography.   2. Holocaust, Jewish
(1939–1945) – Influence.   I. Title.

D804.348.M37 2015   940.53'18   C2015-905671-3

University of Toronto Press acknowledges the financial assistance to its
publishing program of the Canada Council for the Arts and the Ontario Arts
Council, an agency of the Government of Ontario.

 Canada Council   Conseil des Arts
for the Arts   du Canada

ONTARIO ARTS COUNCIL
CONSEIL DES ARTS DE L'ONTARIO
an Ontario government agency
un organisme du gouvernement de l'Ontario

Funded by the   Financé par le
Government   gouvernement
of Canada   du Canada

Canada

For Randi

Contents

Foreword

Margaret MacMillan

If I had to walk through a minefield I would like someone like Michael Marrus to lead me. He is calm, careful, and wise. He would research the location of the mines thoroughly before he moved. As an historian who navigates the complex and highly emotional field of Holocaust history, he is exactly the sort of guide one wants. What he has to say here in this brave and thoughtful book will not please those who want the Holocaust to offer clear lessons that will provide guidance for the future – but his views demand our attention and respect.

Marrus leaves to others the search for moral or ethical lessons from the Holocaust. His aim is at once modest and highly important. While he does not diminish for an instant the horror of the German attempt to destroy Europe's Jews, he says we must try to understand it as an historical event as well as a moral challenge. If we are going to talk about the Holocaust we need to know what it is we are talking about. Without rooting the Holocaust in history we can make assertions about its meaning, as many have, but we deprive ourselves of knowledge in our attempt to understand it. Understanding for Marrus means accumulating as much evidence as possible and weighing the different types of explanations.

He is cautious when it comes to using analogies to link the Holocaust to other historical events. It depends, he says. Analogies are helpful when they open up possibilities or help us raise questions but they can trap us into thinking along rigid lines. He is also wary of single explanations such as Daniel Goldhagen's, who argued that the Holocaust grew out of a deep rooted German antisemitism. As Marrus points out, France and Russia were probably the two countries in Europe before 1914 where antisemitism was at its most virulent but neither undertook the mass genocide of the Jews.

Historians, Marrus argues, rightly in my view, must remain open to alternative possibilities and to complex explanations. And history, he insists, has its own rules and its own demands. He situates himself firmly in the empirical traditions of the English-speaking world. Any claim must be backed by solid evidence. Although he has worked in France on French history, he is not enamoured of the grand patterns so loved by French-speaking historians. Where some of his French colleagues have talked about the duty owed to memory, and about the need to draw clear moral lessons from the past, he remains skeptical of the claims that the memories of those who were there provide an accurate representation of what happened. Memory, as we now increasingly realize, is malleable and subject to change and that is different from history. Others will put up the monuments and the centres to memorialize the past; historians must, as they should, challenge the myths of both memory and memorialization.

It is not easy, however, to consider the Holocaust as we might the French Revolution or the American Civil War, partly because it is still too close to us in time but also because there is something unique about it. It is hard to disagree with Arno Mayer, himself a very distinguished historian, who described the Holocaust, as "a fundamental touchstone of the depth and extremity of the dislocation of Western civilization during the first half of the twentieth century."

The very nature of the Holocaust makes us as humans want to explain it. If we can isolate why it happened, explain why so many ordinary Germans turned to evil, then like doctors finding a dangerous virus, we might hope to find a preventative or even a cure to such an appalling weakness in human nature. Surely, and it is an understandable feeling, such a monstrous event must have lessons; it must offer an inoculation against the future failings of humankind. And surely there must be a redemptive message somewhere. Over the years the need to forestall another Holocaust has understandably become part of the public discourse, used by philosophers, theologians, politicians, or simply concerned human beings.

As the years have gone there have been many attempts to bring out the lessons of the Holocaust but too often, as Marrus points out, what emerges is too vague to be helpful. The mission of the National Holocaust Monument scheduled for Ottawa is to keep the lessons of the Holocaust within the national consciousness. "The hope," says a statement on the website, "is that by teaching current and future generations of Canadians the roots and causes of this atrocity, future acts of genocide will be prevented." Historians have not yet reached a consensus on what those roots and causes are. And they may never be able to. History, as Marrus points out, is an unending process to try to get as full a picture of the past as possible but getting agreement on causes is another matter.

An important part of this book is a history of the process in the past decades to understand the Holocaust and it is also the story of Marrus' own growing absorption in the subject. When he was a student, first at the University of Toronto and then at Berkeley in the late 1950s and 1960s, the term itself was scarcely used and the events themselves barely studied. One of the first great works on the subject, Raul Hilberg's, which was published in 1961, had as its title *The Destruction of the European Jews*. In what is partly his own intellectual biography, Marrus traces his growing absorption in the emerging subject of the Holocaust. He immersed himself in the writing by those such as Hannah Arendt and Emil Fackenheim who tried to come to terms with the meaning of the Holocaust. He followed the debates about whether it was something unique in human history or whether parallels could be drawn with other mass murders of people carried out solely on the grounds of who they were. He was drawn into the arguments about whether some Jews were complicit in their own people's destruction or whether it was the complicity of the rest of the world that allowed the catastrophe to happen. He warns against reading into the past what we now know and reminds us that we have to remember what pressures Jews and non-Jews were facing in their own times. Marrus has always gone to the archives and to the original sources and it is in writing the history that he has made his greatest contribution to understanding.

He doesn't mind moral lessons or admonitions although he prefers to leave them to others. He agrees that we ought to aim to be better as human beings but, as he says again and again, if we are going to use the Holocaust as irrefutable proof to support a particular position we must know what we are talking about. We must also be able to discern when political and other leaders are using the past for their own ends in the present. Prime Minister Benjamin Netanyahu's outburst in October 2015, for example, where he claimed, inaccurately, that the Grand Mufti of Jerusalem suggested the Final Solution to Hitler, is not about getting the past straight but about consolidating political support in Israel and among its supporters in the wider world. As Tony Judt, another great historian of the 20th century, once wrote: "We have attached the memory of the Holocaust so firmly to the defense of a single country – Israel – that we are in danger of provincializing its moral significance."

As the Holocaust has entered the public consciousness over the past half century, especially in the West, we run the risk of drawing lessons that are so general as to be virtually meaningless. Memorials and museums increasingly cast the Holocaust in terms of violation of human rights yet this does not seem a satisfactory explanation for why the Germans murdered so many of Europe's Jews. Sometimes comparisons and lessons are drawn which seem tenuous at best. In the autumn of 2015, the website of the United States Holocaust Museum in Washington compared the refugee crisis in Europe with the plight of Jews in Nazi Germany. And in the so-called lessons there is the ever present danger of trivializing the Holocaust. Recent workshops at the Holocaust and Human Rights Center in Maine discussed bullying and something called ethical literacy.

Does studying the Holocaust teach greater tolerance? Marrus robustly says we must remember that it was about mass killing – something which is very different from intolerance or bigotry. European countries, and Canada and the United States too, had their fair share of bigots in the 19th and 20th centuries but that did not lead to murder on a huge scale. "My principal lesson of the

Holocaust," he says firmly, "is, therefore, beware of lessons." He admits that at best studying the Holocaust can give us a greater appreciation of human reality in all its variety and so it is better than not doing it at all. His own work on the Holocaust has deepened our understanding of what it is to be human as good history must. Exploring the past, he rightly says, is a voyage from which we return wiser than when we left. He has been a wonderful pilot for many years and in this judicious and perceptive book he warns us against the shoals and reefs that can lie in wait for us.

LESSONS OF THE HOLOCAUST

chapter one

Public Lessons and Personal Lessons

Just over half a century ago, in family libraries throughout the English-speaking world, one could probably find, alongside the Bible, a dictionary, and a few other books, an eleven-volume set by a couple, Will and Ariel Durant, entitled *The Story of Civilization*. Somewhat anodyne by present-day tastes, their work presented a celebratory account of the human past. The Durants' history, although never completed (they both died in the 1980s), was a triumph of middlebrow culture of the day, written between 1935 and 1975 in some four million words and covering over ten thousand pages. These books arrived regularly into millions of households via the Book-of-the-Month Club, which included volumes as an inducement to join, and thereby put thirteen million copies into print. The Durants' work became a landmark of accessibility, eventually publishing some seventeen million copies. Recognized by the Pulitzer Prize (1968) and the Presidential Medal of Freedom (1977), the couple achieved great acclaim as masters of a huge panorama of popular history.

Similarly admired was a little volume by the Durants called *The Lessons of History*, published in 1968. Echoing the theme of their larger work, this book was upbeat. Things were improving, despite occasional setbacks. Like *The Story of Civilization*, *The Lessons of History* had absolutely nothing to say about the Holocaust, the persecution and murder of European Jewry during the time of Hitler's Third Reich. Indeed, there was nothing in *The Lessons of History* about Nazism. Nor, so far as I can tell, did anyone ever complain about this omission of what is now considered one of the most important historical events of recent centuries. And nor, so far as I know, did Will Durant's wife and co-author, Ariel, *née* Chaya Kaufman, from a Jewish family from Proskurov in western Ukraine and the granddaughter of a Torah scholar, ever make the case for the inclusion of these terrible events of modern history.

The Durants and their oversight introduce one theme of this book: the lessons of the Holocaust and indeed much else of what we deem to be important in history are not settled matters, as most people might think, but are rather the object of perceptions that differ and that change. Moreover, while opposing views flourish over what to include, contestation is, if anything, even more vigorous when it comes to the lessons of history. I would go further: while these lessons are constantly mentioned in popular discourse, historians generally avoid the issue as an embarrassment, out of keeping with their professional standing. Indeed, the more expert the historians, the more respected they are in their craft, the *less* disposed they are to proclaim lessons of history with any confidence. Put differently, historians and others who know their subjects well are likely to be far more sceptical than lay persons or popularists about the lessons of history – and whether such lessons even exist.

Over the course of some thirty-five years of reading, writing, and teaching the history of the Holocaust, I have contended with the questions that the Durants omitted – what we can learn from the history of the Holocaust. Although the topic of "the lessons of history" has gone somewhat out of fashion, reference to the lessons of the Holocaust is ubiquitous. Unsurprisingly, perhaps. After all, it is about unprecedented horrors: the brutalization of men, women, and children across Europe, in a sinister racially inspired scheme of wiping millions of Jews off the face of the earth; rounding them up everywhere they could be found, often after murderous attacks; exposing them to disease, cold, hunger, and other degrading conditions; robbing them, torturing them, beating them, shooting them, and in some cases murdering them by gassings in trucks or in specially constructed gas chambers, and by the killing of many hundreds of thousands, amounting to close to six million, in all. What should all of this say to us, now that we have had time to reflect and research, over the passage of time? What should we take away, as we say, not only about the events, but about the killers, those immediately responsible, and also those who directed, who facilitated, who helped, who stood by – and for that matter the victims themselves, coming from so many different Jewish cultures, rich and poor, young and old, sick and well, believers and non-believers, scattered across an entire continent in their great diversity?

At the very least, most feel, there should be lessons to learn. Surely we should not be without something that we might use for the world in which we live. It is hardly surprising that so many expect that specific lessons should emerge from exposure to the massacre of European Jewry during the Second World War, and that studying this catastrophe should make these lessons explicit. By lessons, I mean admonitions drawn from investigations of the past – directions that ought to be deduced both from the history of the Holocaust and from comparisons with other state-directed massacres in other situations. Such lessons are not quite the same as "lessons" understood as a portion of Scripture or some other body of material to be studied. Rather, lessons of the Holocaust, in the sense used here, are directions that flow from Holocaust history – the product of research into these matters by historians and others who have thought deeply about the subject.

We hear all the time about these lessons of the Holocaust in public pronouncements by dignitaries and in commemorations and educational contexts. More often than not these are part of public advocacy – as in, for example, "We should heed the lessons of the Holocaust" or "We must not ignore the lessons of the Holocaust" – rather than historical analysis, the kind of talk in which my colleagues and I are likely to be engaged. When I tell people that I am writing about lessons of the Holocaust, they immediately recognize a category and pause, wondering how I can possibly add to what is so regularly alluded to. They may also feel that the topic is hackneyed. Don't we already know the lessons of the Holocaust? From a different perspective, my fellow academic historians usually consider the topic radioactive. Engaging it means messing about in public expectations, or aspirations, rather than historical understanding. My colleagues may also be somewhat mystified because, although we so often hear about these lessons, we have really not thought it worthwhile to probe them very deeply. But I do believe we should. What *are* these lessons of the Holocaust, after all? Is there general agreement about them? Do the lessons differ from one place to another? And do they change over time?

I believe that these questions about lessons go to the heart of Holocaust history and even history in general – in particular why we care about studying the past and what we expect to learn from it. There are many purported lessons out there, and they cannot all have the same transcendent significance or validity. Moreover, the lessons vary a great deal depending on when, where, and by whom they were formulated, and they derive crucially from often-contested interpretations of the Holocaust. For example, some contend that the lesson of the Holocaust is that Jews are always hated, in one way or another, and can only count on themselves. Others claim, quite differently, that the lesson of the Holocaust is that all seemingly well-integrated minorities are vulnerable and require special protection. Which is correct? Can they both be right? And even more important, is there something wrong with formulating in this way what we are supposed to learn from the Holocaust? I think it is interesting that those who are most intensely and systematically involved in the subject have the keenest sense of difficulties in establishing such lessons. That is why, sensing that their competence does not extend to the formulation of such matters, specialists often feel so uncomfortable with them. Similarly, closely related questions probing the prospects of new Holocaust-like catastrophes are seen as awkward. I have certainly watched on many occasions as lecturers try to duck queries about the future or respond evasively about lessons. How many times have I heard speakers protest, as I have indeed myself, saying, "I specialize in the past, and not in the future"?

With non-Holocaust fields, such respectful caution is widely accepted as appropriate. Few historians nowadays will presume to proclaim "the lessons of history" or the capacity to predict the future deriving from a study of the past. Certainly academic historians who venture to do so from their work are likely to be considered either eccentric or hopelessly old fashioned. Occasionally historians might appear who craft some general injunction as an afterthought, but few would wager the authority of their learning in service of such sweeping formulations. And fewer still would dare to propose that these lessons should be universally accepted. One rarely finds modern historians proclaiming historical lessons derived, for example, from the French or Russian revolutions, or the histories of imperialism, gender relations, or whatever. Moreover, for the most part no one complains that such historians are remiss. Audiences usually accept that specialists in these fields have enough on their plates to understand the past without proposing directions for future courses of action based on their particular historical research.

And yet, the public at large seems to be firmly committed to the notion that with the Holocaust it is different, and there are lessons that can be specifically derived from that series of events. Overwhelmingly, people seem to believe that there *are* lessons of the Holocaust that can be reduced to explicit propositions and that Holocaust scholars, of all people, should not shrink from proclaiming them. Holocaust specialists' disclaimers are often dismissed as irresolute, even as indications of moral inadequacy. Many involved in Holocaust education actually agree with such charges. If you enter "lessons of the Holocaust" in Google you will find more than nine *million* hits – certainly more than any willing student, even armed with a computerized strategy, could digest. And if you comb mission statements of Holocaust-related museums, community centres, and memorials you will find copious references to the lessons of the Holocaust. No less an institution than the United States Holocaust Memorial Museum in Washington, DC, highlights teaching these lessons as among its foremost objectives, and entitled one of its recent educational projects *Bringing the Lessons Home*.* The California-based Survivors of the Shoah Visual History Foundation, to take another example, launched in 1994 by the film

---

* Recent Museum draft planning documents that I have seen seem to have removed the commitment to "lessons," however, seeing in the Holocaust rather "a warning that the unthinkable is possible and that human nature makes all of us susceptible to the abuse of power, a belief in the inferiority of 'the other,' and the ability to justify any behavior – including inaction."

director Steven Spielberg, has collected a vast archive of video-taped interviews with Holocaust survivors from all over the world. "By preserving the eyewitness testimonies of tens-of-thousands of Holocaust survivors," the Foundation claimed, this work "will enable future generations to learn the lessons of this devastating period in human history from those who survived." And there are many more examples, some of which I will refer to in this book. People do seem to believe that there are lessons of the Holocaust.

Perhaps one reason for this is that the Holocaust is not like other subjects. The historian Arno Mayer once referred to it as "a funda-mental touchstone of the depth and extremity of the dislocation of Western civilization during the first half of the twentieth century." It is probably the one case of genocide most people can identify. And similarly, as columnist Jonah Goldberg observes, the Second World War may not seem so much like history, because in fact it is the only history about which many people know – or think they know. People may feel more comfortable hearkening to it for les-sons even while they may be wary of applying the unfamiliar ex-periences of far-off times and places. Moreover, I appreciate that many who address the subject have a quite different audience in mind from my colleagues in universities and research institutions. Many who address Holocaust themes regularly promote worthy public objectives to popular audiences, and are prepared to ad-vance hypotheses that extend beyond the evidence at their dispos-al. Also, some who teach in primary or secondary schools may feel duty bound to promote the cause of civic betterment by allowing imaginations to soar and encouraging linkages that evidence can-not necessarily substantiate.

To those who work on the Holocaust in particular, given the sheer, unmitigated horror of the events themselves, there may also be irresistible pressures to find redemptive outcomes – con-ditions that restore one's faith in human decency, or provide illus-trations of exemplary human resilience. And sometimes these can be fashioned into lessons that can be digested and followed. The American writer Susan Jacoby argues that the search for Holocaust lessons may have a religious origin: "the idea that there are some sort of general moral lessons to be derived from the Holocaust is rooted in the religious concept that something good must come out of something bad – that everything, however terrible, is part of a greater plan wrought by an intelligent Designer. Otherwise, how could anyone justify continuing to believe in a benevolent supreme being after such a cataclysm?" Consequently, authorities on the Holocaust may feel that they are expected, even if not in so many words, to present lessons to be derived from their studies. Indeed, to the extent that I participate in civil society, I myself may engage in Holocaust-related public education, commemoration, memorialization, and civic commitments that sometimes associate the Holocaust, for heuristic purposes, with particular causes – most commonly, in the circles in which I move, those of tolerance, anti-racism, humanitarian responsibilities in public affairs, and the like.

Might it also be that audiences are intimidated by claims of lessons of the Holocaust because proponents wrap themselves in the authority that comes from exposing terrible wrongs, to the point that critics dare not push back? We need to remember that those who advance Holocaust lessons often assume great moral authority. And they sometimes do so in an environment facing desperate dilemmas and challenges, including some that entail quite calamitous implications. Does the growth of antisemitism prefigure mass violence against Jews? Should we read particularly violent political rhetoric as prefiguring genocide? How far should we go to aid victims in distress? Should one's country intervene militarily in conflict X or in country Y? An appreciation of Holocaust history can be adduced as a key to resolving such questions. The idea seems to be that guides to correct courses of action lie just beneath the surface of Holocaust narratives, and that familiarity with such material, fortified with moral stamina, will reveal the right path to follow. Naysayers, one can appreciate, hardly feel in a strong position.

I sometimes think about lessons when I see, as I do several times a week at Massey College of the University of Toronto, a lengthy academic injunction that ends, "To be happy, you must be wise." This quotation from the writings of the Spanish-American philosopher and essayist George Santayana completes a lengthy passage inscribed along the perimeter of Massey's dining hall, where gowned students and professors file in regularly, for dinner. To the extent that those present gaze up at this quotation, they may connect not only with its encouragement to learning but also with a related notion, so often applied to the Holocaust that it has come to be taken as one of its core lessons. I am referring to what is probably the best known among Santayana's observations, "Those who cannot remember history are doomed to repeat it." In some quarters Santayana's dictum has come to be thought of as a Holocaust lesson in itself, a warning that a comparable cataclysm might recur if events like the destruction of European Jewry were not "remembered" and its lessons were to go unheeded. Note that, according to the quotation, what is necessary is not to understand, but to "remember" what has happened – although by remembrance is usually meant acquaintance or reacquaintance with terrible injustices and suffering. Moreover, claims of the existence of such lessons are often accompanied by a sense that promoting them is *urgent* – indeed, that inattention to such lessons is likely to prompt terrible consequences. History has spoken, and we ignore her voice at our peril.

This is another, less explicitly descriptive kind of lesson – a suggestion that a close acquaintance with atrocities that happened during the Holocaust constitutes a lesson that should prompt people to behave more wisely or humanely. In Washington, groups of military personnel and police officers constantly tour the United States Holocaust Memorial Museum precisely with this object in mind. I admit to being puzzled about the rationale that is assumed to be operating here. After all, those who are most familiar with the outrages of the Holocaust were the perpetrators themselves – and there is no evidence that a full knowledge of their own wrongdoing ever generated their revulsion against it. In his memoirs, the historian and essayist Walter Laqueur reflected on this theme while discussing how a great part of his life had been exposed to totalitarian regimes in Germany and the Soviet Union. There is no guarantee that such "lessons of history" – that is, persistent acquaintance with cruelty to others – will clarify things one way or another, he observes. In his view, some will emerge from such exposure with a more acute sense of the possibilities of wrongdoing, but some will do the opposite. The lessons of history, like all lessons, "can be misunderstood and misapplied."

Since I have devoted so much of my professional life to the study of the Holocaust, my commitment to its study should be clear. I do not disparage deep reflection on the knowledge we accumulate on this topic, which I believe is one of the foundational events of our age. I believe that the Holocaust is a moral signifier for thinking about good and evil and, perhaps even more important, for pondering what has been called the grey zone, the great space in between. And I also believe that studying the Holocaust contributes to the public good. But I contest the idea that there exist some formulae that constitute lessons of the Holocaust – or even worse, *the* lessons of the Holocaust. In a nutshell, the problem with such lessons is that, unfortunately, history does not speak to the present with so clear an admonitory voice. One of my objectives is to give people pause before they invoke too hastily the authority of the slaughter of millions of people in recommending this or that. And another is to encourage greater respect for the sophisticated understanding of the murder of European Jewry as it has emerged from the remarkable research on the topic conducted by historians in many countries in recent years. I also suggest that this inquiry reveals the complexity of these events and the difficulty of reducing them to neat formulae or recommended courses of action.

In a recent book on the uses and abuses of history appropriately entitled *Dangerous Games*, historian Margaret MacMillan contends that "the past can be used for almost anything you want to do in the present." Her book cautions against the misuse of history, and warns that when we turn to it "for understanding, support, and help," we should do so very cautiously. "If the study of history does nothing more than to teach us humility, skepticism, and awareness of ourselves, then it has done something useful," she writes. "We must continue to examine our own assumptions and those of others and ask, where's the evidence? Or, is there another explanation? We should be very wary of grand claims in history's name or those who claim to have uncovered the truth once and for all. In the end, my only advice is to use it, enjoy it, but always handle history with care." I share these views. We readily acknowledge the truths of these injunctions, I believe, when we think of events that happened long ago, in the very distant past. Most of us accept with equanimity contentions about what we might learn from the Greeks and Romans, the champions of European Enlightenment, or the origins of the Industrial Revolution. There are some hard cases: some modern-day Serbs remain deeply committed to certain conclusions about the Battle of Kosovo in 1389, seen as a pivotal moment for the creation of Serbian patriotism in response to centuries-long Ottoman and Islamic threats and as pointing out with great clarity the dangers that still threaten the Serbian nation. Catholic traditionalists I have met can be quite convinced of the baleful effects of the French Revolution, seen as opening the door to secularism and attacks upon the Church that constitute a continuing danger. Nevertheless, going back in time generally softens our views about the potency of lessons, rendering them less contentious, and in most cases understood as less sweepingly applicable to our own time.

Not so with the recent past. Particularly with human catastrophes, it usually seems to onlookers that the very least we can do in their wake is to distil essential messages from calamities that leave us stunned. Historian Alon Confino addresses the working of what he calls "foundational events" – great caesurae in societies, brought about by events such as the French Revolution or the Holocaust of the Second World War. Foundational events, in his definition, are events of "global symbolic power." Widely understood as of earth-shattering significance by those who live through them, these historical markers are brief, radical, and self-avowedly transformational. As such, they not only command great attention but also implicitly call upon us to understand them. And even more than understand, we often say that people need to *come to terms* with them. For those caught in their grip, this usually means: We want to know what such events "tell us." We want to know "the take-away." We also want those who suffered or those who have perished in the still recent past not to have done so in vain. We seek some good to come out of such upheavals. We want those responsible for associated wrongs to be brought to justice. And we want restitution for those who have been wronged. Hence there follow commissions of inquiry, judicial reckonings with those responsible, the honouring of heroism, restorations of stolen property, and the extending of help to victims and survivors – including listening attentively to them and paying special attention to their explanations of how terrible things might have been avoided. All of these eventually enter a great repository of lessons.

After a while, I believe, this perspective is softened by the integration of catastrophic events into the general stream of history, by an increasing tendency, with the passage of time and generations, to see even the most terrible atrocities as being a part of a wider flow of events, the understanding of which is enriched by debate and discussion, requiring both a balanced assessment and deductions that are in keeping with the historical culture of the day. As well, if the study of a subject is deemed important enough to warrant global, or near-global, attention, immediate perspectives slowly give way to a global vision of justice and understanding – notwithstanding the value and persistence of early impressions and the resolution of particular wrongs. This is what has been happening with the Holocaust.

Writing about this subject in the mid-1980s in my book *The Holocaust in History*, I argued that the Holocaust was gradually entering history, by which I meant that it was residing less and less in the lived memory of participants and those drawn for personal or other reasons to the Jewish catastrophe, and was increasingly being considered as part of the wider history of the Second World War. This has entailed, to my mind at least, not a diminution of attention to it (quite the contrary in fact), but rather an acceptance that Holocaust history should conform to the methodology of the historical discipline: crafting narratives objectively, with due attention to chronology and context; presenting accounts resting firmly on documentary and other evidence; gradually relinquishing material claims against descendants of wrongdoers, as time makes these efforts increasingly difficult if not impossible; and finally, providing explanations that can be tested against generally accepted data – including some that come from other, related events.

Throughout this book I will suggest that this process clashes with the public preoccupation with lessons, and explain why historians of the Holocaust have preferred instead a sophisticated, open-ended, research-driven understanding of the Jewish catastrophe. Looking critically at the lessons of the Holocaust, I believe that, like all history, the Holocaust nevertheless has much to teach us, even when it does not direct us how to solve the problems of our time.

My discussion of the lessons of the Holocaust is very much a personal perspective, drawing upon my own formation as a Holocaust historian and my experience in teaching and lecturing on the subject for several decades. My encounter with serious history writing began in 1959, at the beginning of my undergraduate years at the University of Toronto, more than half a century ago. I was a beneficiary, then, of one of the University's highly specialized undergraduate sequences of study, known as "honours courses," some thirty closely prescribed programs that required four years to complete, as opposed to the less specialized three-year sequences that were called "general courses" or "pass courses." First introduced in the 1870s, these honours degrees included legendary (to me) programs such as "English Language and Literature," "Art and Archaeology," "Maths, Physics and Chemistry," and "Household Economics" (intended for women). For reasons no one seemed to know at the time, seven of these honours courses began with a common first year, known as Social and Philosophical Studies, or "Soc and Phil," as we called it, followed by three more years of broadly defined specialty streams. The latter included Political Science and Economics, Philosophy, and Psychology, among others. My own stream was "Modern History," in which "modern" was quaintly understood to be anything after the fall of the Roman Empire. After a year of "Soc and Phil," a sprinkling of introductory courses in the humanities and social sciences, I found myself fully ensconced in a wonderful introduction to the historical discipline, studying little else but history for three years, and involving very little choice for two years. However, choice abounded in the last of these years, in which we were allowed to select from among numerous highly specialized, year-long seminars of about a dozen students, on very focused topics. Those who taught these courses appeared godlike, and whether we liked them or not, we trembled at the extent of their learning. My choices included John Cairns's "Liberty and Authority: The Nineteenth-Century Tradition," one of the best introductions to European intellectual history I ever encountered, Willard Piepenberg's entire year on the English Revolution, 1640–1660, and a Canadian history seminar given by Donald Creighton, an irascible Canadianist, chairman of the department (a practically inconceivably august level of authority, so it seemed), who reminded us constantly of what peaks we had to scale to get to his level of knowledge of the Canadian past. One might think it natural, in a program such as this, to ask from time to time what might be the practical point of such an intensely specialized program – although I managed to avoid any such reasonable questioning so far as I can recall. Why would I have bothered, I might well have thought? There was just too much to read, and too little time to do so. After a year or so I was hooked.

What I did think about was how I wanted to become a history professor. What better career could there be, it seemed to me, than a lifetime of Modern History with occasional forays back into Soc and Phil – and being *paid* for it! (At that time, the freewheeling sixties, I had not the slightest doubt that I could get a good job and earn a reasonable living from doing just this. Everything changed in the seventies, but that did not affect me directly, for by then I had a post at the University of Toronto, to which I returned with a doctorate in 1968.) I was borne along in a tide of enthusiasm for the discipline, something shared by many of my fellow students in Modern History and most of my instructors. When an undergraduate, I was even invited to a prestigious social group called the History Club, where selected students and their instructors would meet at a professor's home in the evening every month or so, and – guess what? – read papers to the rest, just as we were already doing in our regular program! I should add that, in keeping with the Anglophile culture of the University of Toronto in those days, we were heavily imbued with the work of English scholars and English history, and for that matter the empiricist culture of English academic life, something that may explain my disproportionate reference, in the pages that follow, to the kinds of scholars who particularly influenced me at the time.

After Toronto, I went to graduate school at the beautiful campus of the University of California at Berkeley, from a rather dour environment of changing seasons with plenty of ice and snow, where scholarship was taken desperately seriously, to a sparkling, culturally advanced if somewhat grungy Northern California place of near constant sunshine and political upheaval – "Berkeley in the sixties," as my cohort will always, and usually with great affection and loyalty (certainly so in my case), remember it. The academic tone at Berkeley couldn't have differed more from the Oxbridge-imprinted world I had known in Toronto, and there was not a trace in my new academic home of my undergraduate institutions' somewhat insular self-satisfaction. The Berkeley campus led the parade of cultural and political radicalism of the day, and was among the first institutions to see students mobilized around social and political causes – in our case, American civil rights and Vietnam. I should add that I did, very infrequently, inhale. Much more important, the academic atmosphere was closely interwoven with moral and political contestation, culminating in 1964 with Berkeley's Free Speech Movement, led by a brilliant philosophy undergraduate, Mario Savio.

On a recent visit to its campus to give a lecture, I saw Savio in a photograph in an exhibit in the University's main library, commemorating the demonstrations of the day, giving a speech from the roof of a captured police car – in his stocking feet! The idea was that demonstrators did not want to be seen to be scratching the paint of the vehicle, surrounded by students. I also saw myself in an accompanying photograph. There I am in a sport jacket and tie, regular garb for demonstrating students at that time.

At Berkeley I worked on a master's and then a doctoral degree from 1963 to 1968, broken with a year spent doing research in Paris. (Unfortunately for me, I just missed the French student uprising of May 1968, when I was back in Berkeley defending my dissertation.) In my own cohort we managed to blend radical student politics with serious academic application, and quite unlike in Toronto we were encouraged to read widely outside history and in the social sciences in particular. At least some of this engagement, I can't help but think now, drew me to the Holocaust, a subject that we were just starting to explore through such writers as Hannah Arendt, Bruno Bettelheim, Elie Wiesel, and Primo Levi. To be sure, these were very early days for the Holocaust, or for that matter modern Jewish history. I was certainly not trained as a Holocaust or a Jewish historian in graduate school; and indeed, so far as the Holocaust was concerned, practically no one in Europe or North America was at the time. I personally knew no one, anywhere, who would have claimed such a specialty. Neither university courses nor professors of such a subject existed outside Israel. And there were only the slightest glimmerings of the topic in my readings in Modern History in Toronto or my graduate work at Berkeley in courses and the preparation for comprehensive doctoral examinations. This was still before the time, as the British novelist Ian McEwan puts it, when the extermination camps were "universal reference points of human depravity."

Along with my main focus, the history of modern France, I studied German and other areas of European history with such luminaries at Berkeley as Raymond Sontag, Hans Rosenberg, Wolfgang Sauer, Carl Schorske, Martin Malia, Richard Webster, and Gerald Feldman. While antisemitism certainly had its place in our surveys of modern Europe, and while the Germanists had some feeling for the *Sonderweg*, the allegedly special, authoritarian path of Germany to modernity, nothing in that material that I can recall brought the massacre of European Jewry into our historical field of vision with anything more than vague allusions. Seth Wolitz, a brilliant young scholar of French literature, fresh at the time from the University of Chicago and now retired after having held a chair in Jewish Studies as an authority in Yiddish at the University of Texas in Austin, introduced me to a few French writers who discussed related issues, but almost always in fictional form. Mainly what I recall from his direction were months of being dazzled by his conversation and by Jewish themes in Proust's *A la recherche du temps perdu*, the subject of his own doctoral thesis.

One of the very few books I took with me from Toronto was a well-thumbed copy of *The Origins of Totalitarianism* by Hannah

Arendt, the German-Jewish political philosopher and refugee from Nazism who escaped to the United States in 1941. I still possess this book, about as heavily underlined and annotated as any in my library. I know I read every word, so important did my colleagues and I believe her work to be. I went back to it often, but I will confess that when I did so in the 1990s I found the work practically impenetrable, her prose dense and cumbersome, replete with long-winded, unsubstantiated, and highly abstract formulations. Looking back, I believe her influence had at least as much to do with her treating subjects we thought of essential importance than it did with advancing historical understanding. In my third year at Berkeley I read Arendt's *Eichmann in Jerusalem*, her reportage of the Eichmann trial, which appeared first in the *New Yorker*, and I followed closely the extensive polemics that accompanied her account, centred on both the person of Eichmann and the role of the Jewish Councils, or *Judenräte*, in the destruction of European Jewry. I read other works on the Holocaust as well, but I did not actually put them together in my mind as referring to a single theme, strange as this may seem looking back from our vantage point today. Raul Hilberg's pathbreaking *Destruction of the European Jews*, published by Quadrangle Books of Chicago in a dense, double-column edition of 790 pages, appeared in 1961, but I did not read it carefully until I left Berkeley to return to the University of Toronto seven years later.

I wrote my doctoral dissertation on the Jews of France during the Dreyfus Affair – a topic on which I also drew from some of Arendt's writings. In my thesis, completed in 1968 and published as *The Politics of Assimilation* in 1971, I made a few references to the Holocaust. In the introduction I ventured, somewhat anachronistically I now acknowledge, that as a consequence of their zeal for assimilation, French men and women were perhaps less prepared than they might have been for the catastrophe that came in the war years. So I thought at the time, drawing on Arendt and her brilliant book on the late eighteenth- and early nineteenth-century German-Jewish *salonnarde* Rahel Varnhagen, a Jew who felt haunted by her background. (No student of these matters could have avoided Arendt's brilliant last chapter, "One Does Not Escape Jewishness.")

But my allusions were not much more than that, and the idea of examining the war years systematically never really occurred to me.

After arriving in Toronto in 1968, I worked in social history, a very dynamic field at the time, especially in France, encouraged and guided by my friend and University of Toronto colleague the social historian Ned Shorter, and heavily influenced by Charles Tilly, Richard Cobb, Natalie Davis, and other practitioners of the history of everyday life, *la vie quotidienne*. Eugen Weber, a brilliant scholar of Romanian origin who was then at UCLA, was another important mentor. Born in Bucharest in 1925 and educated at Cambridge University after wartime service in the British Army, Weber was a sophisticated, urbane conversationalist, as well as being one of the most erudite historians I have ever met. A wonderful storyteller, as one of his former students once observed, Weber "had a theatrical, rueful, or mordantly funny quality that characterized his intellectual temperament." I enjoyed many lunches with him at a café near the Bibliothèque nationale on the busy Rue Richelieu in Paris, discussing our most recent findings of the day's scholarly harvest in that wonderful institution. Following Eugen's example, I read widely in French folkloric sources and local history, and published on the histories of drinking, dancing, and local religious expression. One of my topics was the emergence of leisure in the nineteenth century – something of which I had little direct experience in those years.

My academic focus changed abruptly when, a decade after I had left Berkeley, my friend the late Roger Errera, a member of the prestigious French Conseil d'Etat and an editor at the French publisher Editions Calmann-Lévy, approached me from Paris with the idea of joining with the distinguished American historian Robert Paxton, then in his late forties and teaching at Columbia University (and who had briefly been my teacher at Berkeley), to write a history of what happened to Jews in France during the Second World War. The book, Roger insisted, would appear first of all for a French audience. At Calmann, Errera edited a remarkable series called "Diaspora," which had published a French translation of my book on Jews in France during the Dreyfus period, and had brought some major works on Jewish subjects to the French public.

For modern European historians at the time, Paxton was a towering figure: his *Vichy France, Old Guard and New Order, 1940–1944*, published in 1972, was a turning point in the historiography of wartime France, drawing upon German archival material in order to present the French collaborationist regime, in what has been called *la révolution paxtonienne*, as being far more actively engaged pursuing French nationalist and authoritarian objectives than had been customarily believed among French historians, or for that matter the general public. Our book on French involvement in the persecution and eventual deportation of over seventy-six thousand Jews from France, sending all but 3 per cent of them to their deaths, first appeared in French in 1981 and some months later in the United States as *Vichy France and the Jews*. The book was remarkably well received in France and elsewhere, and found an important place in a just emerging Holocaust historiography.

Importantly for my engagement with Holocaust history, the last chapter of our Vichy volume included a section entitled "A Comparative View" that compared events in France with those in other European countries in order to demonstrate the varieties of collaboration in the persecution of Jews across the continent. Our point was the crucial importance of context. Through such considerations, my reflections on the Holocaust in France drew me to subjects as diverse as the refugee crisis of the 1930s, the origins of the Final Solution, the nature of the German occupation, the role of the Catholic Church and the Vatican, Jewish resistance, and many other mainline Holocaust themes. This was my introduction to Holocaust history on a broad scale, and it happened in the late 1970s and early 1980s when the subject as a whole was beginning to take off. Fully engaged by that point, I devoured works on the subject by scholars in Europe, Israel, and North America.

I also travelled a great deal – a logistical challenge in those early years, when my wife Randi and I went with our infant twins, Jeremy and Naomi, born in Toronto in 1973, and later also Adam, born in Oxford in 1979. Our travels began in Paris, where we had a tiny apartment on the sixth floor, *sans ascenseur* (no elevator), and a miniature kitchen without hot water. A few years later we went to Oxford: Randi and I were beneficiaries of the wonderful academic hospitality of St Antony's College (significantly, for Oxford, welcoming women at the time), then under its warden the genial Spanish historian Raymond Carr, and for two years at the end of the 1970s I thrived amidst brilliant colleagues, both locals and other visitors from abroad, splendid scholarship, and – unexpectedly for me – great food and drink. Learning the ropes of high table, I marvelled at the gowns, the college silver, candles, port, and academic ceremony. One result, so far as I could see, was a remarkable degree of civility and stimulating conversation. It was over port and cigars that I met my Israeli friend, the Sinologist Aron Shai, now rector of Tel Aviv University. Oxford's academic dining, my colleagues in Toronto correctly observed much later at dinners I would host when I was an academic administrator, set an example I did my best to emulate. The inspiration I followed was that colleagues who eat well together tend to get along – something of no small importance in academic life.

Jerusalem was another major influence. A few years after the appearance of Paxton's and my Vichy book I participated in a year-long seminar at the Institute for Advanced Study at the Hebrew University, or the "Machon" (Hebrew: Institute), together with Israeli, American, and European academics. Among fellow visitors at the Institute were Yehuda Bauer, Israel Gutman, Dov Kulka, Saul Friedländer, Richard Cohen, Dina Porat, Christopher Browning, and Bernard Wasserstein. We met regularly in weekly seminars, debated major issues of Holocaust history, and received invited outsiders from time to time. From these challenging and stimulating discussions I wrote a book on this emerging historiography, *The Holocaust in History*, first published in 1987 and translated widely. This put me squarely into the international scholarly conversation about the Holocaust, as well as into direct contact with other scholars, teachers, and students from whom I have learned so much, and indeed continue to do so.

From the mid-1980s, I had a clear focus on the Holocaust, both in teaching and publication. Within a few years, scholarship on the subject established an international presence. In 1988, I attended one of the first international gatherings of Holocaust scholars, in

Oxford, called "Remembering for the Future," assembled under the patronage of the gracious, aristocratic Elisabeth Maxwell, of Huguenot background and a promoter of Holocaust scholarship together with her husband, the media mogul Robert Maxwell – a swashbuckling personality, wartime hero, and subsequently disgraced financier. With a great sense of occasion that included luminaries such as Elie Wiesel, Claude Lanzmann, and Franklin Littell, Elisabeth Maxwell brought scores of Holocaust specialists together – not only for academic presentations but also for a spectacular banquet at the Maxwells' Oxford home, Headington Hill Hall. Meetings such as this accented, for me, the international flavour of Holocaust research. As interest in the field intensified, I attended conferences and symposia on three continents, eventually organized quite a few myself, and visited colleagues to lecture at numerous academic institutions. I taught for a year at UCLA in the 1939 Club Chair subsequently held by Saul Friedländer – the first endowed position, I believe, in the history of the Holocaust outside Israel. And it was there that I first met my friend Pierre Sauvage, an Emmy Award-winning film-maker whose documentary *Weapons of the Spirit* broke important ground for understanding the rescuers of persecuted Jews.

The late George Mosse, beloved mentor to so many European historians of my generation, was one of those I saw regularly at this time. Born in Berlin in 1918, Mosse was one of the most senior and respected German scholars of the émgré generation, scion of one of Germany's wealthiest families and head of a publishing empire that included the *Berliner Tageblatt*, one of the most important liberal newspapers in Germany before it was taken over by the Nazis. I met him often at meetings and in Jerusalem – particularly at the home of Hannah and Steven Aschheim, a German intellectual historian and a former Mosse student at the University of Wisconsin. While George, as everyone called him, regularly protested that he was not a Holocaust historian, I always felt his probing of the subject was continuous, if just beneath the surface. Certainly he was an exemplar – embodying the very ideal, for me and many others, of passionately engaged objectivity. Somewhat later I also met and indeed continue to meet with colleagues at the United

States Holocaust Memorial Museum, where I sit on the Academic Committee of the Center for Advanced Holocaust Studies; I assisted the work of Zev Weiss's Holocaust Educational Foundation of Chicago; and I have participated actively in meetings of the history and research commission of the Fondation pour la Mémoire de la Shoah in Paris, now chaired by Annette Wieviorka.

At the beginning of the 1990s, at the invitation of a charismatic English anthropologist, Jonathan Webber, I joined a group of scholars who met on several occasions with Polish museum authorities to communicate Jewish concerns about the public memory of the camp of Auschwitz Birkenau. Meeting first in May 1990 at the Oxford Centre for Hebrew and Jewish Studies at Yarnton Manor, and then at the camp itself, we discussed the huge museological challenges presented after the collapse of the Berlin Wall by hopelessly out-of-date Soviet-era exhibits and historical descriptions, by offended religious and other sensibilities, and by the politically antiquated Polish-national and Soviet interpretations of the history of these camps. Working at the camp complex itself, we gave our perspective to the Polish authorities, and heard theirs. We discussed improvements needed to the dilapidated presentation of that huge camp and prepared for the reception of masses of new visitors from outside the former Soviet Bloc – Israelis, West Europeans, Americans, and others. Our group pressed the case of Jewish sensitivities with the site, something that had been woefully neglected in the past. But from the Museum authorities we heard their concerns – importantly for them, for example, the significance of the Auschwitz camp (not Birkenau) as a symbolic site for the persecution of Poles in the early part of the war, the radically different Catholic and Jewish approaches to burial grounds, and the painful dilemmas concerning some exhibits, like the piles of human hair, that were in a terrible state of deterioration and that should properly, according to some Jewish preferences, be given a proper burial rather than be exhibited publicly. Participants included Serge Klarsfeld, David Cesarani, Annette Wieviorka, Robert Jan van Pelt, Antony Polonsky, James Young, and others. Working through these issues was a crash course in modern museology, involving some of the most difficult issues of group sensibilities and conflicting heritage-related claims. Much of our work coincided with the international controversy generated by a twenty-six-foot high cross put up by a Carmelite convent adjacent to Auschwitz – an issue that remained unresolved for several years and which involved related clashes of perspectives about the symbolic significance of the camp and its ruins.

Towards the end of the decade, I received an invitation to join the International Catholic-Jewish Historical Commission to examine the role of the Vatican during the Holocaust, an inquiry by six scholars, plus two coordinators, Seymour Reich, a senior Jewish community leader from New York, and Eugene Fisher, a leading staff person of the United States Conference of Catholic Bishops with a distinguished background in Jewish-Christian relations. The Vatican's Commission for Religious Relations with the Jews launched this inquiry together with the International Jewish Committee for Interreligious Consultations, or IJCIC (known awkwardly as "itch-kick"), a body with broad Jewish religious, communal, and political representation. The other academic participants were the somewhat prickly historian, the late Robert Wistrich of the Hebrew University of Jerusalem, whom I had known for many years, a down-at-heels Belgian researcher, Bernard Suchecky, who then had a tenuous affiliation with the Free University of Brussels, the quiet and respectful Reverend John Morley of Seton Hall University, author of an important book on Pius XII and the Holocaust, the feisty Gerald Fogarty, SJ, a professor at the University of Virginia and a specialist on American Catholicism, and Eva Fleischner, a gentle, Austrian-born theologian of Jewish ancestry who had been deeply involved in Jewish-Christian dialogues.

Widely understood to be a serious exploration of the role of the Vatican during the Holocaust, our commission's work suffered from a somewhat ill-defined mandate, practically no logistical support, and the absence of any organizational structure whatever. The three Catholic and three Jewish members, living on three continents, were somehow supposed to deal with this complex issue – and in the Vatican's declared understanding at least, were to do so by examining the long-accessible eleven volumes of documentary material edited under the authority of the Vatican's Secretariat of State and published between 1965 and 1981. Before long I received several packages from Rome with all eleven volumes of the *Actes et documents du Saint Siège relatifs à la Seconde guerre mondiale*, bound in blue-grey paper and containing hundreds of documents that had been selected by its Jesuit editors. This was hardly an auspicious beginning. And as it turned out, there were not going to be any surprises. At the end of our work, the Vatican's wartime archives remained firmly closed.

Much of our labour turned out to be a tug-of-war in which the Jewish members, sometimes with the support of some or all of our Catholic colleagues, agreed with the case for an opening of the archives, while the Vatican insisted on limiting the inquiry to the long-available volumes. Still, our discussions of our reading together were generally cordial, free from the polemics that normally accompany this issue. Uncomfortably bound by the Vatican's restrictions, we nevertheless got along, and I at least felt that we learned considerably from one another. In the end the exercise collapsed, following our interim report, which raised many questions that the commissioners felt remained unanswered in the already published material, and called for the opening of the Vatican's archives.

Very little about this inquiry, I should add, bore any relationship to some two dozen commissions that were established by European governments about this time to look into the spoliation of Jewish property and the persecution of Jews in collaborationist societies that were part of the Hitlerian empire. While these commissions differed in scope and structure, almost all were well-funded inquiries by distinguished scholars assisted by research staff. The most important of these, the Bergier Commission that looked into the wartime role of Switzerland and in particular Swiss banks, included historians from Switzerland, Israel, Poland, and the United States, and operated with a budget of some twenty-two million Swiss francs and some twenty-five staff persons in Zurich and Bern. In addition, some forty researchers worked on the project on a part-time basis. The Swiss inquiry enjoyed unimpeded access to public and private archives, and companies were explicitly forbidden to destroy any documents pertaining to the Commission's work. Its final report, published in French, German, and English after six years of labour, was a weighty tome of over five hundred pages that contributed significantly to an understanding of the wartime Swiss situation.

In addition to the Vatican inquiry's internal failings and a lack of infrastructure, our commission was steeped in Catholic-Jewish politics, as we were well aware at the time. There was much talk, in the media and among ourselves, about plans then under way in the Holy See for the beatification and canonization of the wartime pope. Indeed, one of the people with whom we spoke, Jesuit Father Peter Gumpel, was the "relator of the cause" of Pius XII, the official who had spent many years moving this dossier forward to what he fervently hoped would be its successful conclusion. Referring to the Vatican's published collection of wartime documents, Gumpel declared that the issue was open and shut: "Anyone who has read this work can see how the Supreme Pontiff made every possible effort to save as many lives as possible, without any distinctions whatsoever." We disagreed. As to the archives question, it seemed only sensible to see more. On this matter, our commission operated utterly unlike other truth-seeking commissions that were set up at the time, in that ours was explicitly precluded from bringing new archival evidence to bear. The core of our commission's problem, not to mention its credibility, in my opinion, was this limitation to previously published documents. Inevitably, this restriction constantly kept suspicions alive – an unhealthy situation for any loosely articulated body of inquiry, to say the least. Needless to say, these circumstances only increased the aura of mistrust that has dogged the controversy over the conduct of the wartime pope going all the way back to the 1960s.

Nevertheless, I have many fond memories of my time on the Commission, in particular our visit to the Vatican in 2000 and our stay at the Domus Sanctae Marthae, the Vatican's elegantly austere guesthouse adjacent to Saint Peter's Basilica. During our visit I realized how similar, in some ways, the governing structure for over a billion Catholics was to the administration of a large university, something in which I was then engaged at the University of Toronto. The pope was analogous to the president, the cardinals to the vice-presidents, and the bishops to the deans (of which I was then one, back in Toronto). Priests were like the professors, including parish priests and members of holy orders, the latter like chaired professors having more autonomy and sometimes prestige within the structure than mainline members of departments. (Our commission had one of each.) Needless to say, there was plenty of internal politics. Getting all these moving parts to work together was no mean feat. Outsiders to both kinds of institution wrongly assume that authority always flows top down, neglecting the intense deliberations and jockeying for authority that went on laterally and from the bottom up. I certainly learned that in the Vatican, as in the university, people do not all think alike. I have no doubt that not all churchmen whom we met, even at the Vatican, shared Father Gumpel's enthusiasm for the cause of Pius XII, although no one would actually say as much. Hospitality at the Vatican, I have to say, was somewhat meagre – perhaps reflecting Church suspicions about the likely results of our labours.

Still, there were flashes of understanding. The exchange that I remember best occurred when our commission met with Archbishop Jorge María Mejía, the elderly Argentine cleric in charge of the Vatican's Secret Archives, widely respected as a pioneer of Catholic dialogue with Jews. Then the Vatican's chief archivist and librarian, Mejía had taught Old Testament, biblical Hebrew and classical Greek at the Catholic University of Buenos Aires for some twenty-seven years. He had also organized John Paul II's historic 1986 visit to Rome's synagogue, the first such visit by a pontiff in modern times. "What would his Eminence do in our position?" I remember asking him, pressing our demand for the opening of the archives. The Archbishop turned to me with a twinkle in his eye and said, "I would pray, my son."

All of this engagement with Holocaust history has enabled me to ride the great crest of the wave of work in this field that developed with such force beginning in the 1970s. A quarter-century later, following the collapse of the Soviet Union and the opening of archives in the former Communist Bloc, there came a new burst of scholarship, of which so many of us who do not do this primary research ourselves have been grateful beneficiaries. As a result, Holocaust history has matured as a field, associated now with an international community of colleagues, state-of-the-art scholarly resources, a stream of admirable publications, the training of talented and multi-lingual apprentices, and legions of bright, interested undergraduates. Over these decades I have been extremely lucky for the way in which my own interests and opportunities have coincided with an explosion of Holocaust research and writing – but also for the formation that I enjoyed, extending back to my first encounters with the discipline of history at my university, long before Holocaust history existed for North American scholars. My own bookshelves are now jammed with journals, monographs, biographies, surveys, atlases, collections of essays and documents, encyclopedias, and transcripts of archival material. My file cabinets are packed with photocopied articles, collections of clippings, and other material that have survived multiple moves and my periodic struggles to cut back, give away, and discard. And now that I have yielded much of this scholarly terrain to younger and more energetic colleagues, I feel acutely how easy it is to fall behind the vast outpouring of new scholarship, even while I marvel at their ability to keep up.

For several years before my formal retirement in 2009, I enjoyed a platform from which to engage with several generations of undergraduates and graduate students both at Toronto and elsewhere, thanks to the University of Toronto's Chancellor Rose and Ray Wolfe Chair of Holocaust Studies, of which I was the inaugural professor (now succeeded by my good friend Doris Bergen). One of my own ways of dealing with this rapid expansion of the field has been to push in some new directions – in my own case by pursuing a graduate degree in law, which I earned in 2005, and studying Holocaust-related issues of postwar justice seeking and matters of restitution and reparation. And with this, some more good fortune: a series of excellent graduate students who have come my way to write doctoral dissertations on these and related subjects.

This book tells something of the historian who has emerged from my much-appreciated professional background, how the study of the Holocaust has, at least as I see it, matured and extended and evolved into a major international enterprise over the years I have been involved in it, and also, in its main focus, how Holocaust history addresses one of the central claims, that is the lessons, made on its behalf.

chapter two

Historical Lessons

Lessons of the Holocaust call to mind lessons of history, a subject which luminaries have pondered for centuries. Put otherwise, when we commit to the existence of lessons of the Holocaust we are acknowledging a more general capacity to formulate lessons from the past. For whatever else it was, the Holocaust was part of the past about which histories are written, and there should be no reason in principle why some histories should yield lessons and others not. Over the years thinkers have hardly been unanimous that discerning such lessons is possible and that individuals can shape the course of history by applying them. During the Enlightenment some thought deeply about this question because of its radical religious implications. If people could control how history unfolded, some thought, this precluded divine planning or intervention. As late as a century and a half ago, the idea of human agency in shaping historical events was something of a novelty and a contention sharply disputed. Many in the premodern era continued to believe that the course of history was set by Divine Providence, and that individuals could do little to effect particular outcomes. Against this view others sought to formulate a non-theological notion of history, "an ever more complex narrative of secular circumstances, contingencies and changes, [that] has been a principal instrument of the reduction of the divine to the human," as the historian of political thought John Pocock puts it. People could shape the flow of history independently of divine intention, many came to believe, and one way of doing so was to understand and apply lessons of past.

Serious debate turned upon how this might happen, and whether human agency operated with a clean slate, or within fixed parameters. In one tradition, intellectuals invested great energy in delineating predetermined directions of history and speculating about patterns that they discerned. During the nineteenth and twentieth centuries, writers such as Oswald Spengler and Arnold Toynbee produced imposing narratives of the human past; they charted the rise and fall of empires and regimes, examining cycles they followed or trajectories they traversed, often in competition with each other. One of the purposes for constructing these schemas was that people could thereby learn where things were headed – that is, what the future held in store. Other thinkers despaired entirely of being able to deduce such patterns. To them, such grand visions were mythical constructs, and so were claims that one could tease out lessons from what had gone before. Their thoughts on History, with a capital H, could be unpretentiously short, much as those of the great theorists were grand and often portentous. Pressed at the end of his days to tell the world what he understood to be the lessons of history, the great polymath and visionary Aldous Huxley responded with humane simplicity: "It is a bit embarrassing to have been concerned with the human problem all one's life and find at the end that one has no more to offer than 'try to be a little kinder.'" Huxley's comment has a disarming, appealing character. Perhaps we are relieved at the thought that what is asked of us may be simpler than we feared. And that we need not bother to chart the rise and fall of civilizations. Similarly appealing may be the conclusions of the Israeli statesman Abba Eban, who once observed, "history teaches us that men and nations behave wisely once they have exhausted all other alternatives." We like to hear that even the great and famous may lose their way, just like us. Or perhaps, more accurately, that there is no way to lose.

Santayana's famous dictum that "those who cannot remember the past are condemned to repeat it" enjoys, I would say, almost canonical authority, ritually intoned as a warning about *not* learning from the past. Less frequently appreciated is both that Santayana's phrase has generally been torn from its context in his multi-volume *The Life of Reason* and that his intended notion has been challenged by those who have thought deeply about how history can be used. Understood popularly as an admonition to study history so as not to make mistakes in the present, Santayana's observation should rather be taken, say his critics, as an explanation of how we acquire knowledge by retaining past experience, not as an injunction to make use of history for particular purposes. Santayana's choice of the term "remembered" should stand as a warning sign.

As observers have frequently noted, history is quite different from memory, or even collective memory. Pierre Nora, the French authority on the subject, points out that far from being synonymous, the two are frequently at odds. "Memory is life, borne by living societies founded in its name. It remains in permanent evolution, open to the dialectic of remembering and forgetting, unconscious of its successive deformations, vulnerable to manipulation and appropriation, susceptible to being long dormant and periodically revived. History, on the other hand, is the reconstruction, always problematic and incomplete, of what is no longer." The study of history requires objectivity and involves a quest for understanding. What results is a reasoned reconstruction of the past that may well have disappeared from popular memory. It involves the sifting of evidence, comparison, and analysis. Professionally, it depends upon peer review and publication. And it is part of a discourse, among both specialists and amateurs, in which there is a common commitment to truth. Memory is subjective, partial, and is itself subject to changes over time. Memory does not seek so much to understand the past as to *recover* parts of it, and for particular purposes. Memory is cultivated, not constructed. It intrudes, rather than being deduced. It is part of identity, instead of an assessment emerging from debate, comparison, and analysis.

In recent times there has been a great vogue among historians for the study of memory as a means to understand those who remember. Memory, says the French scholar Henry Rousso, "is currently the predominant term for designating the past, not in an objective, rational manner, but with the implicit idea that one must preserve this past and keep it alive by attributing to it a role without ever specifying which role it should be given." Memory "has only a partial rapport with that past," he writes. It is "a reconstructed or reconstituted presence that organizes itself in the psyche of individuals around a complex maze of images, words, and sensations." The psychologist Daniel Schacter adds an additional point: In reconstructing the past, "sometimes we add feelings, beliefs, or even knowledge we obtained after the experience. In other words, we bias our memories of the past by attributing to them emotions we obtained after the experience." And finally, memory, the historian Tony Judt once noted, "is inherently contentious and partisan: one man's acknowledgement is another's omission." That is why it is such a poor guide to the past.

It is not really *remembering* things that happened, therefore, that those who commend Santayana to us have in mind when they see history as a source of lessons; it is rather ruminating on the conclusions that historians draw from their study of the past. And this is, of course, where the problems begin. For as every historian knows, history is subject to *interpretation*, and the effort to derive universally accepted lessons from it turns out to be a hazardous enterprise. This was the earliest lesson I had about the discipline of history, coming from an experience I still recall from my first year at the University of Toronto. One of the glories of the "honours courses" in the first year of Soc and Phil, the program described in the last chapter, was a grand sweep of European history that included a series of lectures given by a distinguished medievalist, Bertie Wilkinson. An eminent constitutional historian who had come to Toronto from Manchester, Wilkinson had a flair for popular history, once broadcasting a series of talks on great personalities in history – Simon de Montfort, Joan of Arc, John Wycliffe, and Oliver Cromwell, among others – over a popular Toronto radio station, CFRB, on Sunday afternoons. I can still recall, after so many years, how impressed I was to hear Wilkinson tell us, in a large lecture theatre, how he had been wrongly criticized in a review of one of his books in the *New York Times*. "He accused me of being an *anachronistic liberal*," he said. I had only the faintest idea of what being a liberal meant in medieval constitutional terms, let alone an *anachronistic* liberal – but what so impressed me at the time was that my professor could be challenged in the *New York Times*, and that historians had disagreements worthy of debate in venues such as that.

Santayana's dictum takes us to the heart of disputations about what can be done with historians' findings. How do we understand the history that is supposed to give rise to lessons? Which interpretations do we choose? And which lessons are applicable to which situations? Have we overlooked some lessons by not asking the right questions? And do we sometimes get the wrong answers? The American historian Arthur Schlesinger, Jr once called the past "an enormous grab bag with a prize for everybody." By this he meant that, as with much intellectual inquiry, if one looks hard enough at evidence one can come up with the answer – or the lesson – that one wants. That is probably why he once insisted that Santayana's oft-quoted maxim is in fact quite unhelpful: "the historian can never be sure ... to what extent the invocation of history is no more than a means of dignifying a conclusion already reached on other grounds." Even worse, considering the authority of some interpretations as a civic duty can close down critical reflection. That is why the popular historian Otto Friedrich once quipped, "Those who cannot forget the past are condemned to misunderstand it."

Examining lessons that used to be drawn from the past reminds us of how, with the best of intentions, our predecessors erred, missing the right cues or shrinking from responses that were thought unpalatable. Geoffrey Elton, the most famous Tudor historian of his day, once provided a striking example. To someone of Elton's background and generation (he was born in 1921 into a family of Jewish scholars named Ehrenberg who fled to Britain from Germany in 1939), no historical issue was more important than the warlike dominance of Prussia and then Germany of the European continent. In his reflections on the historical past, Elton meditated on "that dangerous little phrase, learning from the past." "Owing to two World Wars largely unleashed by imperialist ambitions entertained by successive German governments," he wrote after 1945,

> it is now widely felt that the resurgence of Germany once again threatens the peace of the world. But when, in 1870, Germany was united under

the leadership of that (nowadays) notoriously warlike country, Prussia, the common reaction was very different. That event came after some two centuries of almost uninterrupted aggression by France, and German unification came as the result of a victorious war against that established disturber of the peace. Therefore, at the time and for some time after- wards, the unification of Germany was very widely regarded (outside France) as a most fortunate event, and Bismarck, later converted into a menace, received much praise and admiration.

With the passage of time, therefore, some lessons lose their sa- lience, and other lessons appear. To many observers, what emerges strikingly from history is its inability to predict. "What can history teach us?" asks the eminent French thinker Jacques Ellul. "Only the vanity of believing we can impose our own theories on history."

Historical recollections and the lessons drawn from them are not necessarily salutary appeals to humane outcomes. Aware of this, Margaret MacMillan warns that "there are ... many lessons and much advice offered by history, and it is easy to pick and choose what you want." To many in the world today, the lessons of history are nationalist calls to action – calls to "remember" ancient myths of battles lost or won, martyrdom suffered, or miraculous deliver- ances that keep old enmities alive. And sometimes, even, lessons of history are calls for revenge – with accompanying, sometimes constant fears of imminent annihilation. To this day the Polish in- habitants of Kraków hear from a spire in St Mary's Church in the city's Market Square the haunting sound of the "Hejnał," a sentry's trumpeted call, originating in the thirteenth century, to the citizens of that city warning them that the Tatars were about to attack, and calling upon them to defend their lives by holding off the infidels. (Broadcast at noon on Polish radio, the haunting five notes of this anthem – abruptly interrupted when, according to legend, an ar- row pierced the trumpeter's throat – communicate a message to the entire country, and indeed to the world: Poland is in danger! Understanding these five notes as an emblem of Polish national identity, some even consider the Hejnał as a reminder to the Poles that they are forever threatened by being overwhelmed by some horde or other of aliens. I heard it first with a chill down my spine;

Poles hear it more casually now, like the chimes that announce the arrival of a subway train.) Similar nationalist rallying cries are Irish Protestants' appeals to "remember" the Battle of the Boyne in 1690, when Protestants under King William of Orange held back the forces of the Catholic King James, ensuring the Protestant ascendancy in Ireland; or the cries to "remember" the Alamo in Texas, harking back to the massacre of American defenders of a fortified mission who were slaughtered by Mexican attackers near San Antonio in 1836. As historian Max Hastings writes, "the vast majority of people of all nations, even the most liberal democracies, cherish their national myths too much to want mere facts, or even assertions of historical doubt, to besmirch them. They prefer a nursery view of their past to an adult one, and a host of authors and television producers is happy to indulge them." Those who commend the remembrance of history as a universal norm usually have something better in mind than the cultivation of war cries of centuries past.

History is littered with particular instances in which Santayana's maxim is likely to seem misplaced to historians because the analogies themselves are unable to withstand scholarly scrutiny. The famous Maginot Line, designed in the interwar period to defend France against a German and Italian attack, is a classic example. Named after a French minister of defence, André Maginot, it was deployed by the French, according to the latest military technology of the day, as a network of fortifications, tank obstacles, and other obstructions stretching from Belgium to the Swiss border, behind which their military hoped to mount an impregnable defence along France's eastern frontiers. The lessons of history, in this case the war of 1914–18, so it seemed to the builders of these great structures, were that defence trumped offence in modern warfare. The terrible bloodletting of the Western Front of the First World War, they believed, yielded this conclusion from a careful study of the recent military past – with its trench warfare, crippling artillery barrages, and rail transport of reinforcements. In the event, of course, the Maginot Line was built to no avail: in 1940 the

Germans' innovations in the use of armoured columns and their daring penetration of French territory through the Ardennes forest proved decisive and the French defences were circumvented. The French mistake was not a failure to attend to the lessons of history, at least as those lessons were understood at the time; it was rather that French decision makers proved unable to grasp the innovations in war making that upset the conventional paradigms. Generalized, people may be *too* disposed to draw lessons from the past, rather than the reverse.

One of the most commonly cited lessons of history is that dictators should not be *appeased* – that is, that those threatened with aggression should respond with a credible threat of force, rather than with concessions or peacemaking overtures. This is what is sometimes called "the lesson of Munich," after the 1938 conference in which British Prime Minister Neville Chamberlain gave way to the Germans in their demands over Czechoslovakia, helping to prepare the way for the Second World War. To the public at large there is probably no more powerful set of lessons than those about Hitler and Czechoslovakia – pearls of wisdom deemed unassailable recommendations for statesmen in practically every conflict when war threatens. Historians, I submit, are more cautious than most in defining a "lesson" from this historical episode, knowing as they do that reference to the policy on which it is based itself has a history. Appeasement did not always have the pejorative connotation that we assign to it now, and indeed, from having been understood in the 1930s as a policy of active peace seeking, it only gradually came to be popularly understood as a cringing, delusionary attempt to satisfy aggressors by giving them what they demand. As historians have probed the roots of appeasement, they have deepened our understanding of its original dynamics, certainly understood as more complex in its origins and strategic vision than once was the case. Similarly, our more sophisticated understanding of what happened in 1938 has also made it possible to challenge the idea that there were simple alternatives to policies adopted by those who faced fascist dictators in the 1930s. And so if the "lessons" of Munich are relatively clear about what not to do, they are far less so when it comes to policy prescriptions for analogous situations than one might like. As an analogy, "Munich" remains constantly open to the question of the extent to which it is applicable, or partially applicable, or not applicable at all.

Historians, who should be familiar with the history upon which historical analogies rest, are generally the least comfortable when it comes to asserting their applicability. The more they refine and deepen their understanding of the particular situations historical actors faced, the more they become aware of the difficulties in seeing analogies to other situations, most notably those in the imperfectly understood present. And similarly, the more aware historians are of the conditions under which their fellow scholars write, the more aware they are of how they may miss vital elements of the past. "Events," writes the theorist William Bain, "are transformed into icons of a didactic past that announce our desires, our purposes, and our intentions. They communicate who we are and what we believe." As the present-day idiom will have it, "it's all about us," rather than about an objective, timeless portrait of the past. In consequence, the lessons of history are more often matters of dispute over clashing perspectives, rather than being taken as self-evident.

An additional problem with the use of historical analogies to shape perspectives on present-day problems is the way in which so-called lessons become part of "the unspoken and spoken lore" about a particular kind of problem, a "consensual interpretation," as the political scientist Yuen Foong Khong puts it in his book *Analogies at War*. "At that point," he notes, "analogies step beyond their roles as heuristic devices for discovering new explanations and assume the roles of explanations and facts themselves." Margaret MacMillan refers to one frequently contested American case in the mid-1960s in which this very thing seems to have happened, the Vietnam War. The issue was whether the United States should commit ground troops to Vietnam or withdraw. (In present-day circumstances, this translates into seemingly endless disputes over "boots on the ground.") Lessons, in the Vietnamese case, operated differently on each side of the debate. To the Left, the lesson was that the United States should avoid getting bogged down in a war against a popular insurrection, and indeed that the kind of counter-insurgency such a struggle required was doomed to failure. Their analogy was with anti-imperialist uprisings against the French in Indo-China. But for those on the Right, Vietnam suggested precisely the opposite. In their view what was necessary was to go all out – to bomb North Vietnam and put even more troops into the field. Their preferred analogy was appeasement in the 1930s. "Can't you see the similarity to our own indolence at Munich?" asked American president Lyndon Johnson's ambassador to Vietnam, Henry Cabot Lodge, of his opponents on the left. Sharing this view, President Johnson confessed, "Everything I knew about history told me that if I got out of Vietnam and let Ho Chi Minh run through the streets of Saigon, then I'd be doing what Chamberlain did in World War II." This kind of dialogue of the deaf demonstrates that what is really at issue in such exchanges is not how to handle future conflicts, but rather how to understand the past in order to appreciate the applicability of the "lesson."

One answer to scepticism about the ability to draw grand deductions from history has been to focus on the value of practical experience, keeping in mind the limits of what the past can teach us. Whether the accumulation of such experience constitutes full-fledged lessons is of course another matter. Geoffrey Elton seems to have thought of lessons as a matter of conditioning, a building up of experience, even while discounting explicit injunctions about large choices in human affairs. History's lessons, Elton felt, "are not straightforward didactic precepts, either instructions for action (the search for parallels to a given situation) or universal norms (history teaches that everything progresses, history teaches the triumph – or futility – of moral principles); there is far too much variety about the past, far too much confused singularity about the event, to produce such simple results." However, Elton did feel that "a sound acquaintance with the prehistory of a situation or problem does illumine them and does assist in making present decisions; and though history cannot prophesy, it can often make reasonable predictions. Historical knowledge gives solidity to the understanding of the present and may suggest guiding lines for the future."

The famous American historian Carl Becker was even more modest about predictions, but perhaps more encouraging about values. In his view, the kind of guidance that history provided was not so much the gambler's edge – insiders' knowledge so as to bet on the right horse – than it was to instil a capacity to meet the unanticipated. "The value of history is ... not scientific but moral: by liberalizing the mind, by deepening the sympathies, by fortifying the will, it enables us to control, not society but ourselves – a much more important thing; it prepares us to live more humanely in the present and to meet rather than to foretell the future." A final thought: the deeper one delves into the working of analogies, the more one encounters differences among historians in understanding the past from which similarities are supposed to be divined. In short, thinking by analogy often quite wrongly assumes that the past is a given, and that the real problem is understanding the future. This way of looking at history calls to mind a Soviet-era joke repeated by Tony Judt: A listener telephones "Armenian Radio" to ask about predicting the future. "No problem," is the reply. "Our problem is rather with the past. It keeps changing."

When I studied history in graduate school in the mid-1960s, one of the most cited promoters of the lessons of history was the Pulitzer Prize–winning American historian Barbara Tuchman, whose books on the First World War and comparable international catastrophes drew widespread popular acclaim for their readability and their sober warnings, in the midst of the Cold War, that quite commonplace human blunders could trigger grave diplomatic miscalculations, with horrendous consequences. Of German-Jewish background, the daughter of Maurice Wertheim, who was president of the American Jewish Committee from 1941 to 1943, she was a probing journalist who reported from Madrid on the Spanish Civil War. Granddaughter of Henry Morgenthau, Sr, the American ambassador to the Ottoman Empire during the First World War, one of the earliest to call attention to the slaughter of Armenians by the Ottomans, and niece of Henry Morgenthau, Jr, secretary of the treasury under Franklin Delano Roosevelt, who campaigned during the war for aid to the Jews of Europe, Tuchman might be said to have been disposed by family connections to thinking out of the box when it came to man-made disasters.

Tuchman's *March of Folly: From Troy to Vietnam*, published at the height of America's failed adventure in Southeast Asia, detailed examples of the ravages of human fallibility that seemed particularly pertinent at the time. "Mankind," she wrote, "makes a poorer performance of government than of almost any other human activity. In this sphere, wisdom, which may be defined as the exercise of judgment acting on experience, common sense and available information, is less operative and more frustrated than it should be." "Can we learn the lessons of history?" she pointedly asked. She had her doubts, but she nevertheless wrote in order to help error-prone statesmen of her day manage better. *The March of Folly*, she told her readers, was intended to address "the ubiquity of this problem in our time."

Tuchman's popular volume *The Guns of August*, published in February 1962, a readable study of the blundering path to the First World War followed by statesmen and generals of the day, is said to have played a role in the resolution of the Cuban Missile Crisis in October of that year. Closeted with his aides as the crisis developed over Soviet missiles about to be placed in Cuba, less than three hundred miles from Miami, the American president, John F. Kennedy, cited Tuchman's book as instrumental in his decision making. Having been given a copy by Tuchman's friend, secretary of defence Robert McNamara, Kennedy told his aides that the book prompted him to offer the Soviets a way to avoid thermonuclear conflict. "I am not going to follow a course which will allow anyone to write a comparable book about this time, *The Missiles of October*," the minutes of the meeting record him saying. "If anybody is around to write after this, they are going to understand that we made every effort to find peace and every effort to give our adversary room to move." The goal was to present Kennedy's opponent with a way back from confrontation – in this case a deal in which the Soviets would remove their missiles from Cuba and the Americans would remove theirs from Turkey. I note as well that even if Kennedy didn't really learn from the past, invoking it helped him to explain his decision and lend authority to his actions.

Has Tuchman's "lesson" worn well? One might think so if her lesson was the importance of leaving one's adversary room to manoeuvre. However, one would have to add that the lesson would be banal. After all, few negotiators would dispute that principle today. Moreover, it is doubtful that communicating this bit of wisdom should require the authority of a historical lesson. Armies of lawyers who resolve civil suits could speak knowledgeably about such tactics without ever having known there was a Cuban Missile Crisis or for that matter Tuchman's *Guns of August*. Moreover, it is not at all clear that very many students of history would have seen Tuchman's book as a key to the Cuban Missile Crisis, or would even consider this as one of the lessons of the time. The truth is that we have "moved on," as we are wont to say. During the 1960s, Americans had certain things in mind about the Cold War and how to avoid nuclear war, and we have other things in mind today. Blinkered, clumsy, blundering statesmen seemed fair targets to Tuchman in the early sixties, when Vietnam protests appeared so persuasive in the United States. More often than not, we see the Cold War in quite different terms today. Nowadays, American statesmen have a keener sense of Soviet intentions, and are perhaps less inclined to see the outcome of the crisis as being solely due to an American president having successfully stood up to his Soviet counterpart. Along with blunders, we have a sense, derived from much more information than was available in 1962, of a complex interaction among a variety of players, notably American president Kennedy, Soviet premier Nikita Khrushchev, and Cuban dictator Fidel Castro. To be fair, Tuchman herself seems to have understood that things she wrote in the sixties did not wear so well a half-century later. "History has a way of escaping attempts to imprison it in patterns," she wrote, years after these events. By then, Tuchman was full of caution about defining the "lessons of history," underscoring how "anticipation" seems to be beyond our capacities, and how "prejudgments" block historical actors from seeing the effective way forward.

What has changed since the 1960s is not only the context in which historians write about the First World War and the Cuban Missile Crisis, but our interpretations of these events themselves. These understandings have deepened as historical research has advanced, new evidence has been discovered, and new perspectives have been brought to bear. In both cases historians seem to be backing away from notions of blunders to an examination of habits of mind that imprisoned an entire generation of decision makers in "a complex interaction of deep-rooted cultures, patriotism and paranoia, sediments of history and folk memory, ambition and intrigue," as Harold Evans, for example, writes about 1914.

Understood this way, one of the major impediments to applying lessons from history is the realization that those who made up history's cast of characters were not made of the same stuff as those who act on stage at present, or for that matter in the future. World views change. Cultures operate differently. Leaders face new challenges. What moved some at one time might not in another. Historian Ernest May made this point in a book he once wrote on the application of lessons to the conduct of American foreign policy. During the eighteenth century, he observed, those who cited the past as a guide to contemporary policy thought of human nature as unchanging over time. But change occurred nevertheless. And with it thinkers became less sure about how much we can learn from how our predecessors acted. "Influenced by concepts of evolution, cultural relativism and the like, men have since become uneasy about citing Greeks, Romans, Saxons, or even contemporary foreigners as examples of how they themselves might behave. Also, education has changed, and ruling élites have become more heterogeneous, with the result that people in government are more hesitant about alluding to events or experience outside of living memory." Thereby, students of historical mentalities sometimes warn us, the bottom has fallen out of the way lessons function: because people at the time of the French Revolution responded one way to specific situations does not necessarily indicate that people of our own time will do so. Drawing lessons for 2015, therefore, on the basis of what people did in 1789, 1914, or 1962 becomes a very complicated process indeed, not to mention an extremely hazardous one.

Years ago, in his mischievous way, the British historian A.J.P. Taylor took on the issue of the lessons of history, as his biographer, Adam Sisman, reports in a study of that great contrarian.

A born academic troublemaker who influenced me and so many of my peers who studied international history in the 1960s, Taylor offered a somewhat flippant reason for studying history. "What's it for?" asked one undergraduate, putting this chapter's question to the great man. Taylor was then one of Oxford University's leading and most controversial lights, a man who not only published in popular newspapers but also revolutionized academic communication by appearing regularly on television in its early days, famously delivering lectures, without notes, on a variety of historical subjects. Taylor's reply to the student was classically Tayloresque: "Because it's such fun," he replied. "It's fascinating. Men [sic] write history for the same reason that they write poetry, study the property of numbers, or play football – for the joy of creation; men read history for the same reason that they listen to music or watch cricket – for the joy of appreciation." Taylor loved the irreverent reposte. Typical of the man, however, he left his questioner with something serious, something to think about: "Once [historians] abandon that firm ground," Taylor continued, "once [they] plead that history has a 'message' or that history has a 'social responsibility' (to produce good Marxists or good Imperialists or good citizens) there is no logical escape from the censor and the Index, the OGPU and the Gestapo." "He was what I often think is a dangerous thing for a statesman to be – a student of history," Taylor once said about a famous architect of foreign policy, "and like most of those who study history, he learned from the mistakes of the past how to make new ones."

Years later, another English scholar, the military historian Michael Howard, spoke similarly about the lessons of history at Oxford, although at a formal occasion much more in the idiom of academic respectability. The event was Howard's inaugural lecture as Regius Professor of Modern History in March 1981, when he assumed a prestigious chair endowed by King George I in 1724. Howard's audience – Oxford's vice chancellor and the assembled fellows of the University, among others – may not have known precisely what to expect from him on the subject, but this would certainly not have been the case with his benefactor. In 1724 at least, the record shows that King George wanted an incumbent "of sober

Conversation and prudent Conduct, skilled in Modern History and the Knowledge of modern languages," who would groom "the Youth committed to their care for Several Stations, both in Church and State, to which they may be called." History, the monarch believed, was supremely relevant for this task. Teaching it was how the Regius Professors were to serve the common good.

Present-day readers should note: Howard had no patience with what has become the modern universities' preoccupations with propitiating donors, in this particular case faithfully serving the founder's passions for a particular kind of "relevance." (Admittedly, Howard's donor was completely inaccessible, by 1981, to lawsuits or other protests about the uses of his endowment!) Like his Regius predecessor Hugh Trevor-Roper, Howard did not believe that the job of the incumbent was to familiarize his readers with arcane jargon or to train professionals; rather, his task was to address and to educate laymen. More specifically, Regius Professors were not to worry about imparting the lessons of history to those who would exercise authority. History, Howard told his audience, "whatever its value in educating the judgment, teaches no 'lessons', and the professional historians will be as sceptical of those who claim that it does as professional doctors are of their colleagues who peddle patent medicines guaranteeing instant cures. The past is infinitely various, an inexhaustible storehouse of events from which we can profess anything or its contrary." No ambiguity there.

Possibly even more shocking had these words been spoken before his donor, Howard said that there was no such thing as "history" as a body of truths comprising "what really happened." Instead, "history is what historians write, and historians are part of the process they are writing about." New evidence constantly appears, and even more importantly, the shape of "history" changes with shifts in the historian's *mentalité* and what he happens to be interested in. And so what is known as history is continuously evolving. That is why we should never assume that we will ever settle, definitively, "what really happened," and why the history on which the lessons supposedly rest constantly changes. What is made of this shifting terrain changes accordingly, as new perspectives emerge, new questions are put to the evidence, and new imaginations are enlisted in the effort to understand the past. Historians know these things well, Howard suggested, for the armies of their successors openly assemble; and historians know better than most that "revisions" of their favourite theories and descriptions are only a matter of time. Regrettably for the professors, Howard suggested, lay readers seldom appreciate this. Indeed, this time-limited approach, "for the layman, is maddening." The layman, he continued,

> looks for wise teachers who will use their knowledge of the past to explain the present and guide him as to the future. What does he find? Workmen, busily engaged in tearing up what he had regarded as a perfectly decent highway; doing their best to discourage him from proceeding along it at all; and warning him, if he does, that the surface is temporary, that they have no idea when it will be completed, nor where it leads, and that he proceeds at his own risk.

Quite unlike his Oxford colleague A.J.P. Taylor, Michael Howard was attuned to the expectations of the guardians of the public purse, and in 1981 he was prepared to placate those who expended public funds on universities and history chair holders – even those as august as Regius Professors. Howard acknowledged historians' civic responsibility. But he cast that obligation in terms that George I would probably have found deplorable. Knowing that collective values and social aspirations, understood as emerging from a society's past, shaped policy making in the future, Howard championed the historian's role as guarding that public lore, keeping it safe from propagandists and promoters who would distort public knowledge in the interests of their particular cause or interest. It was the historians' job to keep people honest about the past. "Our primary professional responsibility," he insisted, "is to keep untainted those springs of knowledge that ultimately feed the great public reservoirs of popular histories and school text books and are now piped to every household in the country through the television screens." And of course, had Howard been delivering his message thirty years later, he would certainly have added, perhaps even in a tone of alarm, "through the Internet." What Howard would *not* have said, however, was that historians' predictive capacities have improved with time. "As I always tell everybody," he told an interviewer, "the historian's the last person to ask about the future. We know the record: if we say it's going to happen, it's not going to happen."

True to form, it was the French who elevated the issue of who gets to define an official history to the level of a national debate. While elements of the controversy could be found elsewhere, it was in France that the government attempted to cultivate particular historical memories as a civic duty – hence a phrase heard from time to time: *le devoir de la mémoire*, the duty of memory. And it was in France that opposition mobilized against this effort. Emerging from anti-racism and concerns about xenophobia, and notably an effort to punish attacks on minorities, the "duty of memory" promoted the idea of a moral obligation for individuals, and by extension the state to which they belong, to keep alive the collective memory of particular victimizations. Thereby, the collectivity, sometimes being itself implicated in particular wrongdoings such as the wartime persecution and murder of Jews, undertook to express official contrition over these episodes, often held to be previously neglected parts of national histories. These efforts also illustrate the high stakes that many social groups have in seeing their own communal suffering, often experienced far in the past, validated by the official organs of the state. Associated with the efforts of many to solidify their identities as belonging to groups that have been victimized, members of such groups sometimes believe that they can achieve their communal goals by having their particular victimization codified as official parts of the historical record.

Conflict arose in France over the efforts of government, through legislation, not only to impose particular historical understandings of such matters as colonialism, slavery, the Armenian genocide, and the Holocaust, but even to criminalize "the denial, justification or gross trivialization of such crimes." In 2005, in response to several "memory laws" that sought penal sanctions for abusive writings about particular genocide episodes, a group of public intellectuals launched an association called *Liberté pour l'histoire* – Freedom for History – and engaged hundreds of historians in France, including some of the most prestigious in the country. (In response to an international call for support, I added my name to the many on the list.) There followed vigorous debates and widespread disagreement between the government and these scholars both over the principle of the state assuming a public voice in such matters and over specific interpretations embedded in various memory laws. Such legislation was seen as a challenge to the independence of historians and an effort to politicize matters that should be left to academics and other writers of history to sort out. A *Liberté pour l'histoire* manifesto of 2008 put it this way: "In a free state, no political authority has the right to define historical truth and to restrain the freedom of the historian with the threat of penal sanctions."

The historian Pierre Nora, president of *Liberté pour l'histoire*, denounced the kind of history the legislators seemed to be preferring: "a tendency to reread and rewrite the whole of history exclusively from the victims' point of view," involving "a regrettable tendency to project onto the past moral judgments belonging exclusively to the present without taking into account the change in the times; this being history's very purpose and the very reason for learning and teaching history in the first place." A major flash point turned out to be the effort to mobilize the French parliament to recognize the genocidal character of the massacre of Armenians in the Ottoman Empire. Eventually, these matters were resolved in France, although by no means to everyone's satisfaction, as a result of determinations by parliament and the French Conseil d'Etat, the country's highest administrative court, to put a halt to memory laws. Henceforth the deputies will be able to pass "resolutions" on historical matters, but not laws that carry penal sanctions.

What is important here is not so much the legal status of genocide denial in France, but rather what many felt was the state's usurping the place of the historian.

Quite simply, the memorial laws suggested to opponents that, whatever the motivations of the legislators, they were mobilizing the history of great wrongdoing in order to define historical orthodoxies and to validate the grievances of particular groups. Historians do not generally like the state's interference, through political or judicial proceedings, in matters of historical interpretation, and even less do they appreciate the definition of what can be said about the past through the instruments of criminal law – even if intended to thwart Holocaust deniers. Historians know that history is subject constantly to interpretation, that the focus of history constantly shifts depending upon what questions people choose to address, and they often take it as their role to demystify, rather than to promote, received wisdom – to say nothing of calling such verities lessons. Understandably enough, historians are vigorous champions of free expression in their chosen domains. Partly for that reason, they do not like official histories, histories that mask disagreement behind politically approved versions of the past, or histories that use the authority of government to define official truths. Historians, therefore, often feel nervous about how government and other institutions use the historical past in furthering institutionally defined courses of action.

Count on the pollsters and philanthropic foundations to attempt to define the mood of an entire generation on matters such as the lessons of history. As the millennium approached in 1996, some well-meaning promoters of good things internationally had this very idea in mind. The result was an ambitious and doubtless expensive project – together with paltry results. Looking perhaps for a useful way of marking the arrival of the year 2000 (whatever that meant), an energetic team of future-oriented consultants founded the Millennium Project in 1996, following a three-year feasibility study undertaken by the United Nations University and its American Council, the Smithsonian Institution, and a global health and development consulting firm, Futures Group International. What emerged from these deliberations was "an independent non-profit global participatory futures research think tank of futurists, scholars, business planners and policy makers who work for international organizations, governments, corporations, NGOs and universities," as an early project prospectus had it. This was part of a larger project committed to improving "humanity's prospects for a better future," outlined in a series of manifestos of millennial futurology entitled *State of the Future*. So far so good. A part of the 1996 report was an examination of "Lessons of History." Indeed, those in charge of this high-minded project devoted a chapter of the 1998 project volume to this very subject.

"What are the lessons of history?" the independent non-profit global participatory futures research think tank asked – after starting with their own, somewhat tortured rendering of Santayana, "if the lessons of history are ignored, they are doomed to be repeated" (*sic*). To probe more deeply into the lessons of history, the project's research directors conducted three rounds of inquiry, starting with questions to two dozen or so historians from several countries, chosen from a sample of one hundred names. In the first round, historians proposed lessons and questions about them. In a second round, a more select group of sixteen historians assessed these lessons, both as to their validity and as to their applicability to the future. Then the last word, in a third round, was given to a group of "futurists," who presumably were eager to see what all this amounted to.

A short answer, I think it fair to say, is not much, which is perhaps why the results of this particular inquiry did not, to my knowledge at least, make much of a splash among day-to-day practitioners of Clio's craft. So far as I can see, the Millennium Project, which carries on some of its work to this day, decided to abandon its labours on the lessons of history and has moved on to many other fields. The first two rounds of inquiry identified some lessons – quietly demoted in the text to the term "items" – deemed, in comparison with others, to have "high historic validity" and even "higher future applicability": "Wars in some form will continue," "Some large scale projects turn out to be inefficient," "Communications capabilities are important to survival of political organizations," and "Political systems can collapse suddenly." Other items had "higher historic validity and lower future applicability": "Water shortages lead to social change," and "Epidemics play a great role in evolution of the modern age." And so it went, largely vacuous, unexceptionable generalizations, down to those with lower

historic validity and lower future applicability: "Economic innovations may benefit a society or group, but may have a negative impact on social structure," "Climate changes lead to social
changes," and "Population stability may be impossible." One finding deemed "remarkable" by the authors of the study involved
the "greatest differences" between the historians and the futurists
over a core proposition: "History cannot be used to predict the future." Futurists thought highly of this contention, rating it between
"extremely useful" and "useful most of the time." The historians,
however, had less use for the proposition, with an average rating
close to "Will be true as often as it will be false."

I have struggled with what to make of this finding, and indeed
whether anything can be made of it at all. My two cents would go
with the futurists, sympathizing with their apparent scepticism
about whether historians have any greater predictive capabilities
than anyone else. I have certainly never found this to be the case
and I sense that many of my colleagues would agree – knowing
how unwilling they are to trust the judgment of their fellow practitioners in many other matters. More to the point of this book,
this scepticism casts a shadow over lessons, for without having
a good idea about how things are likely to turn out, one is hardly in a position to recommend one thing or another – let alone
advise others through such a grave set of instructions as lessons
of the Holocaust.

The Millennium Project staggered on beyond the millennium
itself to develop "a concrete action plan ... to relieve the grind-
ing poverty, hunger and disease affecting billions of people," as
its website declares. In 2005 it presented its final recommendations to UN secretary general Kofi Annan, and assigned work to
ten thematic task forces, which in turn presented their own recommendations. (None of these had to do with the history of the
Holocaust, I hasten to say.) I have no idea whether this project will
ever be evaluated, or whether the project's efforts, monitored only
to the end of 2006, will have an afterlife. What I do know is that
those of us who study the past have less and less of an affinity
with the kind of concerted policy work undertaken in this vast
endeavour. Historians have a very different professional culture

from Millennium Project workers, and observers may perhaps agree that whatever valuable achievements may come out of the project, among them will not be a clarification of historiographical problems. Where the Millennium think tank came up short, however, on the uses of history, I believe that the simpler work of historians has been more productive. I turn now to the history of the Holocaust to see how historians have undertaken their own global efforts to understand and to deal with the question of lessons.

chapter three

Early Lessons

Understanding the Nazis' murder of Jewish people took time to sink in – for most people at least – and it took time everywhere, among both victims and bystanders, among those who had been spared the ravages of war and those who had not. Everywhere, it took time for people to put the pieces together. To state the obvious, lessons can only be derived by what is known. During the war, even those directly targeted had difficulty grasping what was happening to them. In occupied countries and within the Reich, diarists and others occasionally found the energy to put Jewish miseries into historic perspective – but such intellectually heroic exercises could barely function amidst brutal persecution, starvation, and massacre. Outside the Hitlerian empire, a small group of activists tried to impress upon governments and anyone who would listen that the Germans' murderous assault on Jews was unprecedented in conception and moral significance. But their numbers were tiny and they made little headway. In country after country, campaigners failed to convince societies and decision makers that what we now call "the Holocaust" was not only an unparalleled atrocity, but also an event of earth-shattering scope and historical significance – and one that might have prompted extraordinary responses at the time.

At the end of hostilities, as terrible scenes of liberated camps horrified many in the West, and even after the pathetic remnants of the Holocaust found new homes, some of them after facing spasms of new assaults and even murder in Poland, the public and their leaders did not really grasp what the remnants had endured and what this vast assault on innocents really meant. Even some who later took up the cause of Jews appreciated little of what had transpired in the camps or killing fields of Eastern Europe. I think, for example, of the thirty-eight-year-old Telford Taylor, a reserve colonel in US Army intelligence who was appointed chief counsel for war crimes at Nuremberg in 1945 and who was to preside over the twelve Nuremberg Military Tribunals, taking on the most important cases tried there under American auspices. Notwithstanding his wartime work on the most secret German communications and his frequent wartime intelligence gathering in Western Europe, Taylor insisted that he did not really become aware of the Holocaust until he studied documents and examined witnesses for the preparation of the postwar trials.

Generally speaking, those who did have a message to relay about what had happened found it difficult to communicate Holocaust themes or put these devastating findings into popular discourse. Both Elie Wiesel and Primo Levi, among the most important authors of Holocaust memoirs, had great difficulty publishing their works. Levi received six rejections of his manuscript *Se questo è un uomo* (*If This Is a Man*), an account of his ten months in Auschwitz eventually recognized as one of the masterpieces of Italian literature, before a publisher took the book in 1947. It finally appeared in a small edition selling fifteen hundred copies and receiving indifferent reviews. As late as 1966, Levi's great work, though better appreciated, did not sell well: that year a flood destroyed six hundred copies of the original edition stored in a Florentine warehouse.

It was not easy for these pioneers of Holocaust writing to get a hearing. Elie Wiesel's experience illustrates the complex passage out of the circle of grieving Jewish survivors in order to address a wider audience. His powerful memoir, *Night* (*La nuit*), one of a trilogy on his Holocaust experiences, first appeared in Yiddish in 1956, more than a decade after his liberation in Buchenwald, volume 117 in a series on Polish Jewry published by a Buenos Aires–based publisher and titled *Un di velt hot geshvign* (Yiddish: And the world kept silent). Written for Jewish readers, *Un di velt* conformed to the conventions of Yiddish-language survivor literature of the

day, both in its obsession with the betrayal of the Jews and its rev-
erential attention to concrete names, places, and details. Two years
later, significantly revised to render the context more general and
stripped of the earlier work's anger and thirst for revenge, *Night*
appeared in a French edition, thanks to its promotion by the eminent Catholic Nobel laureate François Mauriac. The new work,
writes its interpreter, literary scholar Naomi Seidman, positioned
Wiesel within an entirely different literary genre. At the heart of
Nuit was a "mythopoetic narrative" that fitted admirably within a French existentialist discourse on suffering. The young Raul
Hilberg, himself a refugee from Austria who escaped to America in
1939, had a different kind of experience. At Columbia University
in the late 1940s, when he pondered writing his doctoral thesis on
the destruction of the European Jews, he was discouraged by his
prospective supervisor, Professor Franz Neumann, a left-wing activist of German-Jewish background and the author of *Behemoth*, a
landmark study of German National Socialism. No one wanted to
go near the subject, Hilberg learned. "It's your funeral," Neumann
told him. Hilberg felt he was living in a closed world, he wrote in
his memoirs. "I believed I was the only person who was trying to
unearth and describe the German upheaval against the Jews."

Thanks to the recent work of several historians, we now know
about the sometimes extraordinary efforts that Holocaust survivors made, in the immediate aftermath of the war, to document their ordeals and to collect materials that would later find
their way into research institutes and centres of documentation.
Committed individuals, often without any historical training or
professional background, took up this cause as part of a collective
commitment to fulfil the dying wish, among others, of the Jewish
historian Simon Dubnow, murdered during the liquidation of
the ghetto of Riga – "write and record" (in Yiddish: *shreibt un far-
shreibt*). This effort, however, did not extend beyond the boundaries of the Jewish world. And even among Jews there was sometimes
a reluctance or an inability to understand the full significance of
what had occurred.

Historians sometimes say that the lack of awareness of the Holocaust in the postwar era had to do with guilt: Europeans and

others simply blocked their own memory of the victimization of Jews because they sought to hide their own responsibility, either as perpetrators or as enablers. Conveniently, they "forgot" about the recent past. For some, this is doubtless true. But as a sweeping observation about vast numbers of people or, even worse, as a universal explanation, I find this argument unpersuasive. To forget, one must at first have consciousness of something; one has to have some awareness of the thing that has been forgotten. But examinations of wartime opinion have shown how strong was *indifference* to the fate of the Jews. What Robert Paxton and I found for wartime France applies widely elsewhere, I believe: people did not know much about what was happening to Jews because they did not *want* to know. And even when there was some attention paid, what was so often lacking was what we now take for granted, a category that encompassed the distinctive elements of the Nazis' assault upon the Jews. Moreover, this indifference – and occasionally even hostility – persisted, even when the war was over. Opinion polls actually showed quite a high level of anti-Jewish feeling in both Europe and North America in the immediate postwar period.

To my mind, the most plausible explanation of why so many did not think much about specifically Jewish victimization was that they didn't think it particularly important. And not only the Jewish catastrophe; the West turned its back on other killings as well. Thus, in the forced expulsion westwards of some twelve million Germans from East Central European countries, in which an estimated one million Germans died, indifference and even outright repression of the historical record were part of the spirit of the time. As historian Alon Confino notes, "evasion was the norm." Jews, too, could be reticent about what we now call the Holocaust. Outside the circle of family, Jews were often reluctant to speak about the victimization of their people because they feared that drawing attention to the matter might be seen as an unseemly promotion of ethnic particularism. "We all suffered," people were accustomed to saying, particularly in formerly occupied countries, and the widespread assumption was that claiming a higher level of victimization than the norm, or, even worse, blaming neighbours, would only make matters worse for the victimized.

The Second World War, one needs to remind people whose views of that conflict have been shaped during more recent times, was not seen as having been *about* the Jews. "Today we may find such indifference shocking – a symptom of something gravely amiss in the moral condition of Europe in the first half of the twentieth century," declared Tony Judt. "But if we ignore that indifference and assume instead that most other Europeans experienced the Second World War the way the Jews experienced it – as a *Vernichtungskrieg*, a war of extermination – then we shall furnish ourselves with a new layer of mis-memory. In retrospect, 'Auschwitz' is the most important thing to know about World War II. But that is not how things seemed at the time."

Remarkably, this insouciance persisted deep into the postwar years. The French writer Annette Wieviorka notes how survivors of the Holocaust did not assume a significant collective identity. "In the period immediately following the Holocaust," she writes, "survivors did not emerge as a coherent group in any part of society. The Jewish survivor associations that had been created were based on simple ties of sociability and mutual aid and did not harbor ambitions to address anyone except those who had lived through the same experience. The rare efforts they made to bring memory to public attention were largely in vain."

Survivors often circulated their accounts in memorial books among families and the remnants of particular communities. But these memories were not among the stories of persecution and mass murder in the cultural mainstream; they were part of local history, intended as a homage to a time and place that had vanished. For the world beyond, lack of interest persisted. In 1970, historian Karl Schleunes published an important book about the killing of European Jews entitled *The Twisted Road to Auschwitz*. In a lecture I heard Schleunes give not long ago, he reflected on how little people understood about the Holocaust even when his work appeared. To illustrate, he told his audience of how, trying unsuccessfully to find his newly published book in a Chicago bookstore, he finally came across it ... in the *travel* section. Neither Auschwitz nor the Holocaust was, at that early date, associated with a significant historical event.

In Eastern Europe, where masses of people were often themselves victims of atrocities, although admittedly of a lesser order
than those experienced by Jews, indifference continued even longer than in the West, facilitated by Communist ideology and its
political priorities. The failure to register what had occurred was
particularly applicable to the slaughter of the Jews. Tony Judt is
particularly acute on the latter:

> On the one hand, Eastern Europe after 1945 had much more than Western
> Europe to remember – and to forget. There were many more Jews in the
> eastern half of Europe and more of them were murdered; most of the
> killing took place in this region and many more locals took an active part
> in it. On the other hand, far greater care was taken by the postwar au-
> thorities in Eastern Europe to erase all public memory of the Holocaust.
> It is not that the horrors and crimes of the war in the East were played
> down – to the contrary, they were repeatedly rehearsed in official rheto-
> ric and enshrined in memorials and textbooks everywhere. It is just that
> the Jews were not part of the story.

Deeply rooted anti-Jewish sentiment and a storehouse of local antisemitic traditions facilitated this absence considerably – this explains why the removal of the Jews from the wartime history of the
region met with practically no popular opposition, unlike some
other elements of Soviet domination.

For all these reasons, remarkable as it may seem to us, and despite occasional sympathetic references to the wartime genocide
of the Jews, the subject was simply not much on people's minds at
the very end of the Second World War or in the period that immediately followed. Outside the Soviet Bloc there was much less uni-
formity. But even there, when commentators in the West did refer
to the wartime killings, they knew little of what people had gone
through. People rarely singled out the genocide of the Jewish people as different from the victimization of other civilians, or innocents, or minorities. Patriotic sentiments similarly pushed people
to accent a shared wartime ordeal. Sometimes, the murdered Jews
were assimilated with "dissidents," and associated with whatever
larger conclusions people drew from such persecution. Deported

Jews, usually sent directly to the gas chambers, were lumped together in popular discourse with those deported for forced labour. In France, the category *déporté*, deportee, applied indiscriminately to both, and does to this day. Holocaust victims were sometimes memorialized with an official phrase that they were *morts pour la patrie* – had died for the fatherland. Sometimes basic facts of the wartime slaughter were either ignored or misstated.

More often than not, there was little sense of the chronology or geography of what the Germans referred to as the Final Solution of the Jewish Question. The role of collaborating states and governments was also commonly misunderstood. Regularly, concentration camps such as Buchenwald, Dachau, and Bergen Belsen in Germany were assimilated with the death factories in the East such as Birkenau, Treblinka, and Sobibor. American Jews, we now know from the work of historian Hasia Diner, *did* reflect on the European Jewish catastrophe, but the wider society did not, for the most part, follow suit. Although writers occasionally used the word "Holocaust" in descriptions of the slaughter of European Jews, they did not generally do so, and the word was not part of the historical canon. Indeed, outside Israel there was no term that customarily designated what had happened. Raul Hilberg's great book on the Holocaust, the pioneering overview of the subject, appeared in 1961 and was notably titled *The Destruction of the European Jews*. "Holocaust" was not in common use at the time.

At university, students such as myself had no contact with the Holocaust when we explored the history of modern Europe or the Second World War. And indeed, there was no common ground with anything else that I studied. As an undergraduate in the early 1960s, I discovered the historical controversies over which historians were at the time deeply divided. To me, this was an exciting revelation: history, I suddenly saw, was a matter of *interpretation*, and practitioners actually *disagreed* – often brilliantly, in a great British academic tradition – over how events should be understood. I spent hours reading books on the *Kriegsschuldfrage*, the epic contest among historians about the origins of the First World War, and the "Storm over the Gentry" – an elegant but vigorous contest over the role of middling landowners at the time of the Civil War in early modern England. I devoured the disputatious literature on the origins of the French Revolution and explanations of the fall of France in 1940. A publishing venture called "Problems in European Civilization," published by D.C. Heath and Company, all in signature green and white covers (originally red and white), put these debates into conveniently assembled collections of essays, culled from the great works on these topics. The first of these I read was on the famous "Pirenne Thesis" on the early Middle Ages, and others included such highly debated topics as "Innocent III – Vicar of Christ or Lord of the World?" and "The Versailles Settlement – Was It Doomed to Failure?" For undergraduate readers, to have a slim Heath Series book devoted to a topic was a sign that mighty practitioners recognized the subject as fit for professional disputation. I need hardly say that the Holocaust never had a Heath Series volume during my education, and the topic never even came close, at the time, to general scholarly recognition.

This was certainly not due to a lack of standing, in those years, of German history in general or the history of the Third Reich in particular. As a student I read William L. Shirer's bestselling and extraordinarily influential popular work, *The Rise and Fall of the Third Reich*, first published in 1960 – a book that shocked even those who had not read it because of the large white swastika emblazoned on its black dust jacket. Again, this widely read book had hardly a mention of the murder of European Jews. At the University of Toronto, I read a textbook on German history written by a former member of the history department that virtually ignored the persecution of the Jews. At Berkeley a few years later, even with an emerging "identity politics" and with several professors whom I knew who had personal or professional ties to Germany and wartime Europe, the Holocaust had no place in either the great narratives or the broader topics that my fellow students and I studied. Some of my professors and later colleagues were Canadian war veterans, and one of these, a crusty but kindly lunch companion, Colonel Charles P. Stacey, was deeply involved in writing the official wartime history of the Canadian army. When I knew him, he was Canada's leading military historian. But I do not believe he ever wrote a word about the Jews. Certainly we never discussed the matter – and significantly, I never thought to broach the subject with him.

Nevertheless, there were beginnings of Holocaust awareness as far back as the sixties, and I can recall a few works that introduced the subject to me. History students in my cohort considered Hannah Arendt's *Origins of Totalitarianism* as required reading, but that work was difficult, unbalanced, quirky, and without a reliable historical narrative. Arendt only mentioned Auschwitz, and that in passing (referring to "the horrors of Buchenwald and Auschwitz"), and she offered no discussion whatever on the origins of the Final Solution or other topics of Holocaust history. What links to the Holocaust there were – and indeed there were such – came in her lengthy discourses on antisemitism, "the camps," "the killing of man's individuality," the emergence of "radical evil" – all intended to be understood as part of her story of totalitarianism, not the fate of European Jews. I read Elie Wiesel's *Night* in the middle of the decade and Primo Levi's *Survival in Auschwitz* not long after its second English-language printing, in 1968. In the mid-1960s, studying in Paris, I came across the work of a French Jewish survivor, André Schwarz-Bart, who had helped to bring the Holocaust to widespread popular attention in France in 1959 with his prize-winning *Le dernier des justes*, a novel of a Jewish family's persecution and wartime victimization. I recall as well a stunning, partly fictionalized book by Jean-François Steiner, *Treblinka*, a story of the revolt in that camp. I followed a storm of controversy over that book because of its allegations of Jews' complicity in their own destruction – much later the object of a monograph by the then Columbia historian Samuel Moyn. Simon and Schuster published an English translation of Steiner's book in 1967. That year an American radio network producer, Arthur Morse, completed *While Six Million Died*, a book that raised the issue of the failure of the United States to open its gates to prewar and wartime Jewish refugees – accompanied, as publicity for the book noted, by "the most shameful cover-up in American history."

Aside from Hilberg's magisterial tome, Arendt's *Eichmann in Jerusalem* was inescapable: it first appeared as a series of articles in the *New Yorker* soon after Eichmann's trial, and was then revised for a paperback edition by Viking Press, in 1965. (A marker of the passage of time: my copy bears the book's price, $1.65.) The Eichmann trial and a series of well-publicized trials in Germany, in particular the Frankfurt Auschwitz trial in 1963, helped define the emergence of a consciousness of the wartime murder of European Jews that has never diminished. Hannah Arendt's work and the controversy associated with it helped enormously in that effort, even as she herself ironically denounced the use of the Eichmann trial as a vehicle for Zionist propaganda rather than pure justice.

Arendt's work was important, not because it was well-crafted history, which it certainly was not, but because it stirred passionately engaged controversy, raw meat to apprentice historians in the second half of the 1960s, and also because, addressing a wide audience, it linked the murder of European Jews directly to core elements of the history of the time and to passionately disputed Jewish themes. It also gave wide exposure to issues such as the great scope of the Nazis' killing project, the role of the Zionist activist Rudolf Kastner and his rescue efforts in Hungary, the formation of ghettos, the Jewish Councils or *Judenräte*, questions of postwar justice, and many other topics. And then there was her indignant tone – so refreshing to me and my disputatious fellow students in the throes of the student uprising in Berkeley, even as her book aggravated more mature and worldly Jewish commentators. "*Eichmann in Jerusalem* represents Hannah Arendt at her best," wrote Tony Judt, an enthusiast just a few years younger than myself, "attacking head-on a painful topic; dissenting from official platitudes; provoking argument not just among her critics but also and especially among her friends; and above all, *disturbing the easy peace of received opinion* [emphasis in original]." That was the positive view. For her opponents, however, Arendt's presumption was insufferable. "I knew Hannah Arendt when she was a socialist or half-communist and I knew her when she was a Zionist," sniffed her former admirer, Gershom Scholem, the German-born Israeli philosopher and historian of Jewish mysticism at the Hebrew University of Jerusalem, and a close associate of Walter Benjamin and Leo Strauss. Scholem, who had known Arendt in Berlin before Hitler became chancellor, wrote that he was "astounded by her ability to pronounce upon movements in which she was once so deeply engaged, in terms of a distance measured in light years and from such sovereign heights." As these observations suggest, once Arendt threw down her gauntlet, few of those interested in the issues she raised could remain neutral.

Assailing received wisdom, Arendt brought debate on the subject to a large public audience, and did so with characteristically acerbic prose. Most reviewers commented on what they felt was her cold, even heartless exposition. "In the place of the monstrous Nazi, she gives us the 'banal' Nazi," wrote Norman Podhoretz in an attack in *Commentary*. "In the place of the Jew as a virtuous martyr, she gives us the Jew as accomplice in evil; and in the place of the confrontation of guilt and innocence, she gives us the 'collaboration' of criminal and victim." Arendt lambasted the acclaimed Israeli prosecutor Gideon Hausner for seeing Eichmann as an expression of the antisemitism that had wreaked its damage over centuries of Jewish history – and also for being "a typical Galician Jew." His was "bad history, and cheap rhetoric," she opined: the real issue was the mobilization of the Nazi regime by many mid-level, unthinking bureaucrats like Eichmann, all in the service of a modern totalitarian system. Arendt scorned the idea of Eichmann as a monstrously evil anti-Jewish ideologue. In her view, one that has not been accepted by subsequent historians, I might add, the man was utterly *banal*, a blinkered careerist, incapable of understanding what he was doing wrong. And finally, Arendt stigmatized the Jewish administrators set up by the Germans to manage Jewish affairs across Europe, for facilitating the Germans' diabolical plans to regulate, rob, round up, and eventually deport the Jews to their deaths. This was "the darkest chapter of the whole dark story," she wrote provocatively, illustrating "the totality of the moral collapse the Nazis caused in respectable European society – not only in Germany but in almost all countries, not only among the persecutors but also among the victims."

Students with awakened interests in the history of the Holocaust thought much, almost certainly too much, about Arendt, it can now be said, but I was certainly not alone in considering issues she raised as compelling matters for debate, something that had been sorely lacking on this subject in my formal education at Toronto and Berkeley. Critical reviewers of Arendt – most were critical – included some of the most vigorous writers on contemporary Jewish affairs (there were relatively few Holocaust specialists then): Lionel Abel, Oscar Handlin, Norman Podhoretz, Marie Syrkin, and others. Arendt had a hard-hitting public exchange of letters with Gershom Scholem, who famously denounced her lack of *ahavat yisrael* – love of the Jewish people. Arendt replied that she did not love any people – only her friends. Jacob Robinson, a Lithuanian-born Jewish civil servant based in New York who had advised the Israeli prosecution, published an entire book on the subject of Arendt's errors, pointedly entitled *And the Crooked Shall Be Made Straight* – part of a verse from the book of Isaiah. Legalistic by training and temperament, Robinson found plenty of factual mistakes in Arendt's work, but he couldn't hold a candle to her in the cut and thrust of polemical dispute. For three years during the mid-1960s, debate was intense and discussion ranged in scores of publications.

All of this was grist for the mill for those such as myself who had never read much on the history of the Holocaust. To Jews outside Israel, according to historian Idith Zertal, the trial and the polemic associated with Arendt's book about it "became inextricably connected and of one piece." Even today, as evidenced most recently in Professor Deborah Lipstadt's book about the Eichmann trial, it is difficult to separate the proceeding itself from Arendt's analysis of it. The subject, for me at least as I was discovering it, touched upon issues of vital importance, not just for contemporary Jewish self-definition, but for the course of modern history from which it had previously been excluded.

In retrospect, the subject of communities in the works of social thinkers such as Jane Jacobs, Seymour Martin Lipset, Nathan Glazer, and others attracted much attention during that era, along with a keen interest in civil rights, discrimination, and racism. These writings helped to generate inquiry into Jewish assimilation and the effects of oppression on other minority groups – only a short intellectual hop to work on Jews' experiences of victimization from antisemitism and their interactions with Nazism. My own

doctoral thesis of 1968, an examination of French-Jewish assimilation at the time of the Dreyfus Affair, drew upon such sources, and
was marked as well by my reading of Arendt and also Proust's
Remembrance of Things Past, one of the formative literary examinations of modern identity and socio-cultural stratification. All this
underpinned a growing interest in the victims of the Holocaust –
in memoir literature, with works such as those of Elie Wiesel and
Primo Levi, but also in path-breaking overviews.

For me, the most important of these was Isaiah Trunk's massive
Judenrat, a well-researched study of the German-imposed Jewish
Councils in the ghettos of Eastern Europe. Among the most promis-
ing of Jewish scholars in prewar Poland, as the Polish-Jewish historian Samuel Kassow has described him, Trunk escaped the Nazis
by fleeing to the Soviet Union, and later lived in Poland, Israel,
in the Israeli Kibbutz Lochamei Hagetaot (the Ghetto Fighters'
Kibbutz), in Calgary, Alberta, and finally in New York, where he
eventually became chief archivist of the Jewish Research Institute
or YIVO. A prolific writer in Hebrew and Yiddish, Trunk conscien-
tiously combed the terrain that Arendt had examined so superfi-
cially in her Eichmann book.

Trunk documented how the leaders of the Jewish Councils facilitated much of the persecution and killing process, but this happened often under threats to their lives or enticement with false
promises by the Germans, the mix differing in different situations.
He charted the sometimes agonizing choices of the Jewish leaders and the Jewish police, and documented their transgressions in
some cases, but he was far more attentive than Arendt to their often
limited options. "The Councils ... faced a tragic dilemma never before experienced by a community representative organ," he wrote.
But then came "the morally dangerous borderline of collaboration."
Some Councils and their chairmen crossed that line. Some sent the
children first, or prepared lists of deportees. Or saved favourites.
Or succumbed to bribery. Others resisted, even to the point of suicide. Some even aided young clusters of Jewish resisters. Unlike
Arendt, Trunk was interested in what has come to be called "the
grey zone," the field of action in which moral choices are not always clear. The roots of Jewish behaviour, he suggested, lay deep

in Jewish history. Jewish collaboration with their oppressors during the Holocaust was an extreme example of conduct that Jewish community leaders had, in desperate times, seen as the only way to prevent even worse things from happening. Unlike Arendt, who boldly fitted the conduct of the councils into her theory of totalitarianism, Trunk ended his book with the historians' conventional call for more research. The behaviour of the Jewish Councils was analogous to, among other situations, that of the community leaders in Tsarist Russia in the first half of the nineteenth century. More work was needed to establish precisely how. No one, after reading Trunk's hundreds of pages of detailed evidence, could ever accept Arendt's sweeping denunciations of the Jewish Councils without at least some second thoughts. The lessons, if lessons there were from the story of the Jewish Councils, would never be quite so clear as many found them to be in her argumentation.

Media events in different countries stimulated long-forgotten wartime memories. In France, Marcel Ophuls's extraordinary documentary *The Sorrow and the Pity* (in French: *Le chagrin et la pitié*), exploring collaboration and resistance through numerous interviews and with important material on the persecution of the Jews, was originally commissioned for French television in 1969 but was banned from the airwaves until 1981 – partly on the urging of Simone Weil, a prominent, right-of-centre French Jewish politician and Auschwitz survivor who argued that its message was too one-sided. Much later, Ophüls told the story of how the director general of the ORTF, the French television network, found his way to General Charles de Gaulle, then in retirement at Colombey-les-Deux-Églises, to complain that the film had been blocked for showing "disagreeable truths." "France does not need truths," the General is supposed to have replied, "she needs hope." The film nevertheless was released for commercial distribution in 1971, shown widely in cinemas, and had a great impact on the French public. Histories that track the eventual corrosion and collapse of the wartime and postwar Gaullist-inspired myth of a German-initiated persecution of Jews look back to this film as an important step in that process.

In a class of its own was the French public intellectual Claude Lanzmann's path-breaking nine-hour film *Shoah*, completed in 1985 and often thought to be the greatest Holocaust film of them all. Omitting archival footage, photographs, or contemporary testimony, this epic presentation drew exclusively upon the filmmaker's interviews with survivors and participants, nudged or bullied or enticed by a Lanzmann obsessed with detail. Notwithstanding the latter's interpretative one-sidedness and his irritatingly heroic presentation of himself, *Shoah* is an astonishing work, which made a brilliant case for the singularity and horror of the wartime murder of the Jews. Still, for historians, whose vocation it is to *understand* the past, *Shoah* sounded a sour note: not only was Lanzmann's film *not* a work of history, as he often explained, but he also had no use at all for historical explanation, context, or analysis. In Lanzmann's view, the Holocaust could *not* be explained or understood in the manner of professional historians, and attempts to do so were doomed to failure. We know all we need to know about it, he seemed to be saying; what we need is to *experience* its horror and face what was done to its victims. As to lessons, Lanzmann had nothing to say. His film, he told the French newspaper *Libération*, was "the incarnation of the truth," the very opposite of "the sanitization of historical science."

Not long after the film's appearance, I found myself in Lanzmann's presence at a retirement luncheon for Raul Hilberg at the University of Vermont. Lanzmann spoke on that occasion. I have no recollection of his speech, and hardly any of the event itself, but it is plain from his own writing that Lanzmann felt deeply aggrieved, at that time, by professional historians' assertion of "their mandarin prerogatives and their status" when commenting on his work. In his view, the historians were in a state of panic before his great accomplishment and his courageous, selfless portrayal of the truth. In Lanzmann's memoir, *The Patagonian Hare*, he mentions that I sat at his table at lunch, and that I "felt hounded from [my] kingdom." He goes on to say that my "dark beady eyes glared poisonously at [him] throughout the meal." I recall nothing of this, although I can attest that my eyes are not dark. When I read this comment, some years after the event, I was reminded of Lanzmann's prodigious capacity to see almost every situation he considers as part of the world's running commentary on himself.

Holocaust awareness seemed to thrive on controversy, despite
the fears of many that divergences of view were indecent, a grave
threat to public memory. Certainly the longest-lasting dispute was
the furious debate that continues to this day over the alleged "silence of Pope Pius XII" during the Holocaust, triggered by a play,
The Deputy, written by the German Protestant playwright Rolf
Hochhuth and performed in 1963. And there were many other contentious events, about which people still argue. These included the
waves of panic throughout the Jewish world prompted by the 1967
and 1973 wars between Israel and her neighbours and accompanied by widespread anxiety about the survival of the Jewish state;
the impact of Elie Wiesel's writings in the 1970s and his insistence
on the "uniqueness" of the Holocaust; NBC's highly popularized
1978 television mini-series, *Holocaust*, watched by close to 120 million viewers; and much later, in the mid-1980s, the polemics centred
in Germany over the so-called *Historikerstreit* or historians' debate,
pitting Right against Left on the place of Nazi crimes and the murder of European Jews in contemporary German life. Other disputed landmarks included the publication of Lucy Dawidowicz's
extraordinarily successful *War against the Jews* (1975), emphasiz-
ing a single-minded early intention on the part of Hitler and the
Nazis to murder the Jews, the convocation of several international
historical conferences that highlighted different interpretations of
events, and a lively dispute over a book by David Irving claiming Hitler's ignorance, until 1943, of the Final Solution. (This was
considerably before Irving morphed into a full-fledged Holocaust
denier, for which he was exposed in his failed lawsuit against
the American historian Deborah Lipstadt and later sentenced to
prison in Austria.) Gradually, as the term "Holocaust" came into
widespread use, the wartime massacre of the Jews was increasingly conceptualized, debated, commemorated, and memorialized.
Historians and others began to publish well-researched books on
the subject, intended for a growing audience of interested readers.
Since then, historical inquiry has proceeded apace – enriched, I believe, by debate and differences of interpretation – to the point that
it is probably impossible, now, for a single person to master all of
the literature that appears. But to what ends? Commentators agree

and disagree. And as they do so, accompanying their work, there are often passionate discussions of lessons.

Hannah Arendt's work on Eichmann occasioned one of the earliest and most powerfully articulated lessons – namely, that an imminent threat to mankind lay in the prospect of modern bureaucracies spinning out of control to produce something new in human history: "administrative massacres" in which "this sort of killing can be directed against any human group." For Arendt, the fearsome lesson of the Eichmann trial was her seemingly perverse claim that the significance of the Holocaust had very little if anything to do with the choice of victims. Although Arendt supported the Israelis' undertaking to try Eichmann, as many did not, her critique of the proceedings in Jerusalem was resolutely universalist. Arendt abhorred the idea, formulated in Israeli law, of narrowing the trial's issue, as she saw it, to "crimes against the Jewish people." The correct path, as she put it, was a trial for "crimes against mankind committed on the body of the Jewish people." Essential to her analysis was the advent of the new kind of crime formulated at Nuremberg, "the crime against humanity – in the sense of a crime 'against the human status,' or against the very nature of mankind." In her interpretation this crime was "an attack upon human diversity as such, that is, upon a characteristic of the 'human status' without which the very words 'mankind' or 'humanity' would be devoid of meaning." Eichmann embodied the kind of criminal who was essential for the carrying out of such a crime, and what was remarkable about him as he went about his murderous business was his utter banality. In conflict with what subsequent historians have actually discovered about Eichmann, Arendt believed that the man was "thoughtless," lacked any imagination, had no idea that what he was doing was wrong, and indeed *"never realized what he was doing* [emphasis in original]." By "thoughtless," Arendt did not mean stupid; she was using a Kantian concept – thoughtlessness as the opposite of ethical awareness. As she concluded, "such remoteness from reality and such thoughtlessness can wreak more havoc than all the evil instincts taken together which, perhaps, are inherent in man – that was, in fact, the lesson one could learn in Jerusalem."

To her, the identification of this characteristic was what was new and particularly horrifying about Eichmann – not to mention horrifying about Hannah Arendt, at least to many of her readers.

It is emblematic of the malleability of "lessons of the Holocaust" that just a few years after Arendt had popularized this notion of a new threat for all mankind, another German Jew, Emil Fackenheim, reached a radically different conclusion about what the wartime Jewish catastrophe signified, and what were its lessons for the present. Fackenheim's work had an enormous resonance, to the point that he became, in North America at least, the most eloquent articulater of a Jewish quest for meaning after the Holocaust. I became acquainted with him when I returned to Toronto as a newly minted academic in 1968. Speaking with a thick German accent and, much later, with a beard that recalled engravings that I saw as a child representing biblical prophets, Fackenheim was to me at least the very image of Jewish *gravitas* – and this notwithstanding his lively sense of humour and occasional irreverence so long as the subjects did not involve the issues that consumed him at the time – mainly the Holocaust, antisemitism, and Israel. Engaged in the left-liberal Student Christian Movement, he and his wife, Rose, a former student, later a convert to Judaism and the more radical of the couple both on Jewish matters and liberal causes, opened the door of their home to ecumenically orientated Christian theologians and opponents of antisemitism. Understandably enough, the latter was particularly important to the couple, but for reasons I never really grasped Fackenheim's particular obsession was the antisemitism that he found in the United Church of Canada periodical the *Observer*, and its editor, Rev. A.C. Forrest – betraying a lack of everyday political proportion I was not alone in seeing later in his politics, particularly on Israeli matters.

Born in Halle, Germany, in 1916 and ten years younger than Arendt, Fackenheim received Reform rabbinic training in Berlin during the mid-1930s. After finding refuge briefly in Aberdeen, Scotland, he was sent to Canada in 1940, where he was interned in a remote camp near Sherbrooke, Quebec, as an enemy alien, together with other German-Jewish refugees from Nazism. Among his fellow internees, in Quebec and elsewhere, were the writer and broadcaster Erich Koch, Erwin Schild, a conservative rabbi, and the distinguished Catholic theologian Gregory Baum. Upon release, Fackenheim served for five years as a congregational rabbi in Hamilton, Ontario, and then, after completing a doctorate in philosophy at the University of Toronto, taught mainly German philosophy there for more than three decades. During the early 1960s he was deeply involved in a project, never completed, on the philosophy of religion from Kant to Kierkegaard. Then came a radical break. Largely uninvolved with Holocaust issues prior to the end of that decade, he experienced a major shift in his thinking about that time, probably sparked by a meeting with Elie Wiesel at a conference on religious ecumenism assembled by Rabbi David Hartman in the Laurentian mountains near Montreal. Wiesel later described how the German-born survivor shocked the participants by raising the subject of the Holocaust. For Fackenheim, whose friendship with Wiesel dates from that meeting, this was the most important intellectual transformation of his life.

In his 1968 book *Quest for Past and Future*, Fackenheim describes his "great discovery," part of his awakening to "the scandal of Auschwitz." A unique event in Jewish history, the Holocaust posed deep questions about Jewish survival.

> Not until I faced this scandal did I make what to me was, and still is, a momentous discovery. Jews throughout the world – rich and poor, learned and ignorant, believer and unbeliever – were already responding to Auschwitz, and in some measure had been doing so all along. Faced with the radical threat of extinction, they were stubbornly defying it, committing themselves, if to nothing more, to the survival of themselves and their children as Jews.

Thereafter, writes one of his former students, Michael Oppenheim, Fackenheim's role would be to take on this commitment, "translating responses of the community [to the Holocaust] into philosophic and theological language." One of the earliest to ponder the philosophic significance of the wartime massacre of European Jewry, Fackenheim came to the notion that, whatever else it taught, as Michael Morgan, a close friend and one of his most distinguished interpreters puts it, "the authentic response must oppose it and cannot either let it be or, God forbid, support it." "Any genuine working through of a return to Auschwitz," writes Morgan, must involve

> an obligation to oppose it, and that means to do what one can to make its repetition impossible – to oppose hatred of Jews, to serve the cause of human dignity, to oppose fascism, and more. The horrified surprise that arises when one confronts inexplicable evil cannot remain surprise or mere thought; it must become resistant action. Hence, a genuine confrontation with the Holocaust and an authentic cultivation of memory results in an obligation to opposition.

Essential for the Jewish world, and for those who sought postwar lessons from the horrors of wartime atrocities against Jews, Fackenheim's particularistic admonition was utterly at odds with the thinking of Hannah Arendt. For the Jewish philosopher, as opposed to Arendt the universal thinker, the Holocaust was a historically unique event, an encounter with radical evil, a decisive break in Jewish history after which the world "can never again be the same." Following this attempt to eradicate the Jewish people, the lesson of the Holocaust was that, thereafter, *Judaism* had to survive and thrive. Fackenheim articulated the point negatively as the 614th Commandment – to be added to the 613 *mitzvot*, commandments held to be given by God to Jews in the Torah and authoritatively compiled by Maimonides. Fackenheim's commandment: *thou shalt not give Hitler a posthumous victory.* He called this "the commanding Voice at Auschwitz":

> We are, first, commanded to survive as Jews, lest the Jewish people perish. We are commanded, second, to remember in our very guts and bones the martyrs of the Holocaust, lest their memory perish. We are forbidden, thirdly, to deny or despair of God, however much we may have to contend with him or with belief in him, lest Judaism perish. We are

forbidden, finally, to despair of the world as the place which is to become
the kingdom of God, lest we help to make it a meaningless place in which
God is dead or irrelevant and everything is permitted. To abandon any
of these imperatives, in response to Hitler's victory at Auschwitz, would
be to hand him yet another, posthumous victory.

As Morgan explains: "It was [Fackenheim's] way of saying 'no,' of
making resistance, courage, and opposition to threat emblems of
Jewish pride, and of showing how the Holocaust could be confronted honestly and yet, in a sense, transcended."

Students of Fackenheim have pointed out how the essentials of
his Holocaust lesson were all in place before his first articulation of
the 614th Commandment at a symposium in New York in March
1967. The chronology is of interest, because the subsequent event
that gave energy to his cause was the Six-Day War in the Middle
East that broke out shortly thereafter. That spring, Egyptian president Gamal Abdel Nasser mobilized the Egyptian army against
Israel and proclaimed his goal to annihilate the Jewish state. At
the beginning of June, Israel pre-emptively went to war against
Egypt, Syria, and Jordan. The result was, in Fackenheim's view, a
miraculous Israeli victory.

To the raw material of philosophic reasoning, the Six-Day War
imparted to Fackenheim and to many other Jews whose "lessons"
are described in this book a chilling anxiety – something that had
largely been absent from Jewish public life since the end of the war.
As Israel's neighbours mobilized against her, there seemed a real
prospect that the Jewish state and people might be destroyed. The
theologian Rabbi Abraham Joshua Heschel, one of the most prominent Jewish voices of his era, described the instinctive and widespread Jewish linking of Israel's peril with the Holocaust: "Terror
and dread fell upon Jews everywhere. Will God permit our people
to perish? Will there be another Auschwitz, another Dachau, another Treblinka?" "In those days many of us felt that our own lives
were in the balance of life and death," he continued, "that indeed
all of the Bible, all of Jewish history was at stake, the vision of redemption, the drama that began with Abraham."

Fackenheim suddenly found himself at the very centre of Diaspora Jewish thought. Events brought the chilling issues of Jewish survival during and after the Holocaust together with the vulnerability of the Jewish state. Notably, the Jewish philosopher now castigated the Christian churches for their silence during both the Holocaust and the Six-Day War. Speaking of Israel but likely referring to the Holocaust as well, Gregory Baum, a close associate of German-Jewish background and a convert to Catholicism, suggests that "Fackenheim's extraordinary inner turmoil during and after the turning-point seems to be related, in part at lest, to his own previous prolonged inattention."

"What [the Six-Day War] added," concludes Morgan, "was support for [Fackenheim] personally and a receptive audience to hear his utterance. In part it was able to provide that audience because Jews in America were immersed in a period of shifting identities, and the fragmentation of American commitments was encouraging group affiliation and identification and a questioning for rootedness and particularity. Confrontation with Jewish memory seemed dramatically appropriate at a time when the Jewish people had been singled out, forced both to 'return into history' and to find a way to survive in history all at once." However interpreted, Fackenheim's articulation of the 614th Commandment and his writings on Israel had extraordinary resonance in North America at the time. He managed, as his friend Louis Greenspan puts it, "to address the Jewish people as the thinker best able to translate their collective experience into philosophic concepts." In support of this argument, Fackenheim insisted on the manner in which the targeting of Jews for eradication corresponded with their unique role in history – a theme of uniqueness that he later developed more fully in his book *To Mend the World*.

There was a sad sequel: Fackenheim moved to Israel in 1984 at age sixty-eight with his wife, Rose, then not yet converted to Judaism and a driving force in their decision, according to friends. Shortly after they arrived, Rose began showing signs of the dementia that would end her life prematurely, in 1989, at age sixty-two. Unlike North Americans, Israelis did not have a visceral connection with Fackenheim's thought. His romantic, emotional embrace of the Jewish state found little echo in the country. Isolated in Jerusalem, never having fully mastered Hebrew, and remarkably without an intellectual following in his new home, Fackenheim was, according to Greenspan, who visited him there in the 1990s, quite alone. And so there was a tragic element in his move to Jerusalem – but perhaps something heroic as well, as Rabbi Dow Marmur, a critical admirer, once wrote about him. Contrary to all warnings about philosophers trying to live out their philosophy, he moved to Israel, and suffered for it.

Holocaust-related events in the 1960s also saw the emergence of an accusation of complicity in the destruction of European Jewry that continues to our own time. This genre, together with its inescapable implication of lessons, focused not on the destruction process itself but rather on the failure of the Western world to respond. As historian Peter Novick noted in his 1999 volume, *The Holocaust in American Life*, the topic of the world's indifference and consequent abandonment of the Jewish victims "had been discussed from time to time since 1945, but almost exclusively in internal Jewish talk; they didn't figure much in remarks directed to a gentile audience." Arthur Morse's *While Six Million Died* was one of the earliest of such works, certainly the first that I read, and even while it concentrated on the latter part of the war rather than the decade of the 1930s, it set the tone for accusations of the failure to help Jewish victims, in this case the unwillingness of the American government to expend any effort to assist Jewish refugees or to open the gates to American refuge. Morse prominently referred to those responsible – in his view US president Franklin Roosevelt and his principal associates – as "bystanders," a term that would echo in Holocaust historiography up to our own time, increasingly carrying a pejorative message: the world had *enabled* the Nazis to carry out their wartime massacre. From this emerged an entire school of thought devoted to a Holocaust lesson, awkwardly borrowing from Fackenheim's original formulation: *thou shalt not be a bystander*.

Various books on this theme followed in the next two decades and beyond. Their titles reflect their message. David S. Wyman published *Paper Walls: America and the Refugee Crisis 1938–1941* in

1968, and its sequel, *The Abandonment of the Jews: America and the Holocaust 1941–1945* in 1984. Monty Noam Penkower's 1983 book was called *The Jews Were Expendable: Free World Diplomacy and the Holocaust*. (Pushing in somewhat a different direction were works with simpler, explanatory titles, reflecting less harsh or judgmental assessments: Henry Feingold's *The Politics of Rescue: The Roosevelt Administration and the Holocaust 1938–1945*, which appeared in 1970, and Richard Breitman and Alan Kraut's *American Refugee Policy and European Jewry, 1933–1945*, in 1987.) Other important works were Bernard Wasserstein's *Britain and the Jews of Europe 1939–1945*, which came out in 1979, and that of my Canadian colleagues Irving Abella and Harold Troper, *None Is Too Many: Canada and the Jews of Europe 1933–1948*, in 1982. These are just a few of many works, which now extend to critical investigations of France, the Scandinavian countries, Spain and Portugal, and even, very recently, the Soviet Union. For my part, I will add my own book, a general survey but one that seeks to put Holocaust refugees into a context of many other European refugee movements: *The Unwanted: European Refugees in the Twentieth Century*, which appeared in 1985.

Although these interpreters differed, as historians customarily do, their works offered variations on a common theme – the history of inaction, indifference, and insensitivity. To me, however, there has always been an important question of how far one should take this analysis. David Wyman's sharp critique of the indifference and expediency of the Roosevelt administration and also of what he felt was the timorous response of the mainline Jewish community was unsparing. "Without impeding the war effort, additional tens of thousands – probably hundreds of thousands [of Jews] could have been saved" – a point vigorously disputed by the distinguished Israeli historian Yehuda Bauer, who emphasizes the iron determination of the Nazis and the priorities of global warfare. And, just as important, their capacity to realize their murderous goals. Quite apart from the difficulties of measuring might-have-beens in history, Wyman's line of thought entails important difficulties in dealing with hindsight, as many critics have pointed out over the years.

As I tried to explain in my book *The Holocaust in History*, the pitfall here is one that tempts any who seek to derive lessons from terrible things that have happened in the past. This is negative history, the history of what did *not* happen. With negative history, critics can make sense out of calamitous events by adopting the standards, value systems, and vantage points of the present, rather than of those who faced catastrophic situations. Sometimes they adopt the perspectives of tiny groups of contemporary critics, who we can claim in retrospect to have been correct in some of their views, but who at the time ignored the outlooks of overwhelming numbers of their countrymen and women. Down this road lies a loss of perspective that ultimately drains our capacity to understand why people actually did what they did. At worst, such work descends into an angry, self-righteous lament that the people being written about did not live up to our standards. As I have described it, this approach is the historian's form of hubris: to yield fully to it is to denounce historical actors for not being like ourselves. The American politician and self-professed historian Newt Gingrich seems to have been at least momentarily afflicted with this disposition when he once proclaimed, "People like me are what stand between us and Auschwitz."

Sometimes too this approach can promote a closed victim's narrative that turns in on itself, in which the historian or the seeker after explanation, faced with what he sees as baffling evidence of inhumanity, falls back upon one of a series of propositions for which there is no evidence beyond the case being examined: that people will *always* turn their backs upon victims; or that people *generally* prefer to do nothing; or that *all that is necessary* for the worst to happen is that good people do nothing; or that hateful, bigoted words *regularly* lead to great atrocities; and so forth. The problem with such propositions and such lessons is of course that inhumanity does not always occur; neither Jews nor anyone else are always victims; stigmatization does not invariably lead to the worst; and conversely vigilance cannot guarantee that dangers are correctly perceived; and so on.

An opposite pitfall frequently yawns, best expressed by the well-known adage *tout comprendre c'est tout pardonner* – to understand all is to forgive all – variously attributed to Spinoza, Tolstoy, or Madame de Staël. Historians must do their best to check this temptation as well, as most I believe are well aware. The most prudent injunction, it seems to me, is to find a balanced way forward – the product of good judgment, common sense, and as much knowledge of context as it is possible to bring to bear. This was the course I tried to propose when I first discussed this issue in *The Holocaust in History* – that historians accompany their outrage with a conscientious, sometimes painstaking effort to enter into the minds and sensibilities of those who acted in the past. With the Holocaust this is particularly recommended, given what both survivors and witnesses assure us was a fundamental experience of those who lived through that time: the utterly unprecedented character of the catastrophe. "It was like another planet," say those who faced the Nazi atrocities. "We simply could not believe it," say both the victims and the bystanders – or better still, "we could not *imagine* it." To a degree, contemporaries were all in the dark. All the more should we take special care to give what they say a fair hearing. Survivors and bystanders alike, these men and women of the past are like delegates from another world. The beginning of wisdom is to listen carefully to what they have to say.

The United States Holocaust Memorial Museum opened its doors to the public in Washington, DC, in April 1993, accommodating many elements of Holocaust consciousness that had been evident since the end of the 1960s. Prominently situated on the Mall, this sombre building, created by architect James Ingo Freed, powerfully evokes the exhibits within and has become not only an American but a global beacon for the study of the subject. An American government institution, the Museum participates in the continuing debate and development of Holocaust memory, and also enjoys sufficient standing for many to seek its imprimatur on decisions about Holocaust issues and interpretation. The Museum has also been one of the world's phenomenal institutional success stories, welcoming nearly thirty-eight million visitors over the past twenty years. Thirty-four per cent of its visitors are school-age children, 12 per cent come from abroad, and approximately 90 per cent are not Jewish. In addition to its formidable regular exhibition, the Museum organizes special presentations, travelling exhibits, and in-house education projects – all of which deliver information via the most up-to-date digital technology. It boasts a publishing program, perhaps the world's largest Holocaust library, important documentary and photo archives with many materials not found elsewhere, and substantial film, video, and oral history collections. There is a Center for Advanced Holocaust Studies, a program of scholarly visitors, and a senior scholars' division that is a leader in the field. I have followed its successes and challenges carefully, having been a member of its Center for Advanced Holocaust Studies since 1999.

Emerging from a Holocaust commission under the presidency of Elie Wiesel established by American president Jimmy Carter in 1978, the project of a Holocaust memorial began with much more emphasis on commemoration than on education in general or on "lessons" in particular. Almost from its inception, Jewish representatives and those who came from East European communities divided over the degree to which the events to be memorialized were to be mainly about Jews (a position that came to define itself as involving six million victims) or to include as well a purported five million non-Jewish victims (thus encompassing eleven million victims in all). Once ignited, this controversy defined the deepest disagreements over what the project was all about. Non-Jewish ethnic groups insisted that a memorial should acknowledge millions of "Slavic" victims of the Nazis, notably Poles, Ukrainians, and others. Jewish representatives feared that if the commemorated were to be "victims in general," the special significance of the place for Jews would be forgotten. Their argument was that the victimization of Jews was unique, historically. Opposing lines hardened.

How could this quarrel, referred to by Edward Linenthal, the Museum's historian, as "the struggle for ownership of Holocaust memory," ever be resolved? Elie Wiesel insisted on the uniqueness of Jewish victimization during the Holocaust, even as he sought to reach out to other victim communities. By the autumn of 1979, Jewish supporters rallied to the idea of a "living memorial" to the Holocaust whose boundaries were somewhat fluid, but drawn mainly around the story of the six million Jewish victims. Interestingly, among the supporters of the cause of eleven million victims was none other than Simon Wiesenthal, an obsessive, Vienna-based Nazi hunter and a lone wolf among the Jewish promoters of Holocaust memory who persistently attacked Jewish leaders who differed with him on the issue. Born in Buczacz, in Austro-Hungarian Galicia and what is now Ukraine, Wiesenthal survived several German camps during the war and was liberated from Mauthausen by the Americans in May 1945. Having lost most of his family to the Holocaust, he spent much of the remainder of his life in Austria, tracking wartime murderers of Jews – often in high-profile efforts for which he became both famous and controversial. In the late 1970s, Wiesenthal had an epic quarrel with Wiesel over the number of Jewish victims of the Holocaust that descended into bitter personal recrimination. Israeli historian Yehuda Bauer believes that Wiesenthal had no strong evidence for his claim of five million non-Jewish victims and that he simply invented it in order to ingratiate the Jews with non-Jewish communities who also suffered great victimization. Among Wiesenthal's critics, his Israeli biographer, Tom Segev, presents this as a strong possibility as well.

What is clear is that this quarrel over numbers appeared increasingly unseemly to those in the American government responsible for launching the Museum. A somewhat exasperated White House declared its choice in 1980, claiming that "'the Holocaust' is the systematic and State-sponsored extermination of six million Jews and some five million other peoples by the Nazis and their collaborators during World War II." To be sure, this was not the end of the story, for as time passed plans for the Museum that emerged from Carter's Executive Order shifted. As Linenthal put it, "language used to define the Holocaust in 'official' correspondence changed according to the interest of the writer and the intended audience." Those concerned seem to have worked hard "to lessen, rather than widen, conceptual distance between victims." The last definition that he notes in his book is a White House revision of the Museum's presidentially appointed Council's mandate defining the Holocaust as "the systematic murder of six million Jews, and the murder by the Nazis of millions of others representing a score of nationalities during World War II." Appreciated only, perhaps, by specialists, the word "systematic" represented an effort by the White House to move towards the Jewish claims of the uniqueness of the Holocaust. Gradually, the disagreements subsided, with the emphasis, if not the formal determination, being on the singling out of Jews for mass murder.

Once the museum project was launched and its prominent location on the Mall established in the early 1980s, planning faced a blizzard of lessons it was supposed to teach. For the American government, the Museum had an important message to convey about the United States' role in the world to promote democratic values and to stand in the defence of freedom – symbolized in the building by the prominent place given to the flags of American military units that liberated concentration camps in 1945. In 1983 some linked these distinctively American themes to the Cold War, then at a moment of heightened tensions, a position taken by Republican columnist George Will. His argument was that the Museum would be a counterweight to American innocence, teaching the public about how dangerous the world could be. But there were also opponents of the so-called "Americanization" of the Holocaust. Some of these charged that the Museum would wrongly credit the United States' role on behalf of Jews when in fact, as one critic said, the government "refused to lift a finger to halt the Holocaust or open our shores to the few survivors." Linenthal provides a convenient summary of other perspectives. Columnist Tom Braden argued that the Museum would be able to resist the misuse of history for nefarious ends, "a form of murder of Holocaust memory." Moralists claimed that the Museum "would remind Americans of the dangers of being bystanders, it would teach Americans where Christian antisemitism could lead, and it would impress upon Americans the fragile relationship between technology and human values. Some supporters insisted that the museum would provide a crucial lesson in individual responsibility." Others saw the main lessons as dealing with the perils of bureaucratic management, or the need to take personal responsibility in the face of pressure from the state, or the idea of connecting the Holocaust to social concerns or civic virtues. Additional lessons included calls for vigilance internationally and a warning against the spread of hatred and dehumanization or other forms of victimization.

Linenthal wisely applies to the Museum the metaphor of boundaries: the institution drew lines "both firm and permeable around a way of remembering the Holocaust." "Official memory would authoritatively define the Holocaust, provide evidence for its uniqueness, and determine what events, if any, might be compared to it and remembered alongside it." Official memory would also define "the 'Americanization' of the Holocaust, the attempt both to link Americans to the story and to highlight professed American values through stark presentation of their antitheses in Nazi Germany." Today, when the Museum enjoys high standing for its many activities and its authoritative articulation of Holocaust lessons, it seeks to articulate as close to a consensus about these issues as can be achieved. The Museum, notes its website, proclaims "a powerful lesson in the fragility of freedom, the myth of progress, the need for vigilance in preserving democratic values. With unique power and authenticity, the Museum teaches millions of people each year about the dangers of unchecked hatred and the need to prevent genocide." As it does so, the Museum's boundaries are regularly tested, as groups or individuals seek to enlist the institution's support in registering their claims for its recognition. For the most part, the institution has maintained a consensus view, advised by accomplished scholars, judicious staff members, and those on its presidentially appointed board, the United States Holocaust Memorial Council. But this has not stemmed the tide of lessons, which continue to beat against institutions of public memory, making it virtually certain that these will gradually evolve with the passage of time.

Is what has been achieved by the Museum a definition of success? Coming at the end of the Cold War, the Holocaust Museum floated on a tide of optimism. To many at the time, at least, aspirations for the institution were very high indeed. As one commentator has written, "Holocaust education was to be a gift from the Jewish community to the world at large." Lessons would be taught. People would come and learn. Genocides might be prevented – or if not prevented then reduced in extent or shortened in duration. In journalist Sam Schulman's shrewd but ironic observation, "there is something ineffably '90s about the enterprise. Vice President Al Gore – an iconic '90s figure – explained how it was to work in a speech on the first anniversary of the museum's opening: 'In order to prevent such an atrocity from ever happening again, those who care must tell the story.' Give me a child, the Holocaust education movement said to the world, and after passing through my exhibits and taking one of my courses, I will give you back a woman like Samantha Power or a man like Warren Christopher or even Kofi Annan – a warrior against future genocides, or at least a person immunized forever against racism and the desire to murder thousands of civilians with the stroke of a pen."

To my mind, these caustic observations are more than a bit too demanding – although perhaps no more so than the lofty ambitions that accompany most great humanistic enterprises. There is a better standard, and that is how well the Museum and so much else that is a part of Holocaust education contribute to human understanding. Since the Holocaust happened, and shocked the conscience of humanity, people are going to study it. The itch to understand is part of the human condition, "so deeply ingrained is our need to 'make sense' of even the most 'senseless' calamities," writes Michael Bernstein, "and so powerful is the urge to enfold even the harshest experiences within a recognized pattern." And when people strive to do so, they owe it to themselves, not to mention to the memory of those who suffered and died, to be as faithful as they can to the events themselves. That is what victims themselves sought and what I think is a laudable collective enterprise. Consider the alternative, giving up the effort: surely this would be much worse. People make this effort and seek to do it well, whether to set their minds at rest, or to mend the world, or to achieve through explanation what some will take as a measure of justice – and they do so in each case by not allowing silence or ignorance to have the last word.

chapter four

Jewish Lessons

Should accounts of the Holocaust pay more attention to its victims? Israeli scholars have often said yes, while others, for example German historians, have chosen to concentrate on the perpetrators. The question is important, because it concerns not only how we understand what happened but also what, according to some perspectives, we might learn from these different accounts. Over the years, some have made the case that the persecuted are best placed to teach us about radical evil. The most famous of these victims, the teenager Anne Frank, whose luminous diary recounts her experience hiding in Amsterdam from the summer of 1942 to the summer of 1944, when she was captured by the Germans and deported to her death, has moved millions of readers around the world since its first publication in 1947. In 1999, *Time* magazine named Anne Frank one of the most important people of the twentieth century. But in another view, some insist that what we really need is to understand how mass murder happened, and that our attention should focus mainly on the perpetrators. Their argument is that the experience of victimhood is tragically common. What is distinctive about the Holocaust, they say, is the particularly obsessive character of the Nazi regime when it came to Jews, and the unprecedented way in which perpetrators attempted to snuff out the life of every Jew they could find. To those who believe in lessons, this debate is important: it governs not only where we will look for them but also what those lessons are likely to be all about.

Holocaust historians have gone back and forth on this issue, in some cases extending the hunt for evidence so as to obtain the most complete picture possible of how the process of mass murder actually worked. Among the most skilful and deliberate efforts to achieve this, Saul Friedländer's two-volume history *Nazi Germany and the Jews, 1939–1945* has broken new ground in its blending of first-hand accounts of Jews, targeted for persecution and murder, with a more traditional presentation of Nazi policy and its perpetration. But it is not easy to strike this balance – and exceptionally difficult to do it well. More than once I have seen distinguished historians of the subject taken to task for relying excessively on documentation that has come to us from the perpetrators, who, in the case of the Nazis, often generated reams of material about what they had done.

The late Raul Hilberg, dean of Holocaust scholars of his day, was sorely criticized for drawing almost exclusively on German records when he wrote his path-breaking *Destruction of the European Jews*, and the relatively few pages he included in that book on the Jewish response to Nazism received the harshest criticism of his work. Those of us who knew him were almost invariably sympathetic to his case, I believe, because we appreciated his great achievement in our field. Hilberg almost singlehandedly brought the wartime murder of European Jews to scholarly respectability, painstakingly tracked the Germans' "Final Solution of the Jewish Question" using the great mass of documents assembled by the Allies at Nuremberg, and also mentored leading scholars who followed in his wake. His great and lasting contribution was to understand the massacre of European Jewry as a vast, coordinated enterprise, in which tens of thousands of bureaucratic perpetrators played essential parts. After outlining how Nazism built this machine, Hilberg described how it ground away on a continental scale, destroying the lives of (as he calculated – always conservatively) just over five million Jews. Everything in his book went back to this notion – and to the authority of the documentation that described how the bureaucratic machine worked, and why it was central to the Germans' killing program.

In public at least, Hilberg was the least sentimental of scholars – and this was certainly so with regard to victims of the Holocaust. He was never one to defer to victims' testimonies, about which he was extremely wary. To him, the story of Jewish reactions flowed from his general perspective on the efficiency of the Nazis' machinery of destruction. This approach brought down upon Hilberg all kinds of charges of having misunderstood or disparaged the work of Jewish leaders and having falsely attributed to the Jews a centuries-old culture of political passivity and evasion. In a short memoir, *The Politics of Memory*, published in 1996, he defended his views on the subject of Jewish victims, clearly in a mood to settle scores with his critics. In his dry, spare prose, Hilberg cited various slights that he had experienced at the hands of the Israeli commemorative and research institution, Yad Vashem – even describing how he was *persona non grata*, for a time, at that institution's archives. As he recounted, the opprobrium persisted for years, largely unabated. It took nearly a half a century for Hilberg's book to appear in Hebrew, finally published by Yad Vashem as if in penance for snubbing the master so many years before. Although he eventually patched up his relations with the Israelis, Hilberg continued to bear a grudge for what he had suffered. The chapter of his memoir describing the reception of his great book in 1961 is entitled "The Thirty-Year War."

I knew Hilberg reasonably well in the 1980s and 1990s when he was at the height of his authority as the master of the German documentary record. An émigré scholar – Hilberg's Austrian-Jewish family had come to the United States from Vienna via Cuba when he was thirteen years old, arriving on September 1, 1939, the day of Hitler's invasion of Poland. Having served in the American army at the end of the war, he attended Brooklyn College and then Columbia University, where he received a doctorate. Later, he taught political science at the University of Vermont until his retirement in 1991, without a stable of graduate students but with a devoted and engaged following outside his home institution. He died in 2007, aged eighty-one. A grumpy, brooding presence in his public persona, peering through large 1970s-vintage glasses and conservatively dressed in a black suit and a white shirt, he was an imposing, unsettling figure – a man of few words in conversation, but someone whose pronouncements seemed to me to define the conscience of the field. At the same time he was almost painfully shy – seeking to avoid conversation, as my wife Randi remembers when we had him to dinner in Toronto. He had little time for popular exaggerations. "The Philistines in my field are everywhere," he once wrote. "I am surrounded by the commonplace, platitudes, and clichés."

Having completed his great book at the end of the 1950s – published in 1961 with considerable difficulty after an adverse assessment by Hannah Arendt, who believed that previous studies had already exhausted the subject, plus an opinion from an Israeli reader that the manuscript ignored Hebrew and Yiddish sources – Hilberg continued to work away with the documents, but never produced a sequel or took on another large-scale subject. After the passage of nearly a quarter of a century, he published a new edition of his *Destruction of the European Jews* in three volumes and 1274 pages. Reviewers paid homage to the author's original achievement, but some were unhappy with the new version, complaining that it had not incorporated recent research, and that in particular Jewish victims had been given short shrift.

In 1992, Hilberg published a short overview of his work on the Holocaust, *Perpetrators Victims Bystanders*, his first work to follow the big book's revised edition of 1985. This new volume appeared in his characteristic style: outward calm, with flat, unadorned prose, enlivened only occasionally by his taste for bitter irony. Reviewing *Perpetrators Victims Bystanders* in the *New York Times*, I was generous with praise, I thought, but I couldn't hide my disappointment. Here is what I said:

> Mr. Hilberg finishes without a conclusion, as if to say that there is no last word. Yet since his "Destruction of the European Jews," and particularly over the last two decades, historians have added greatly to our understanding of the Holocaust. New questions are constantly being asked, new documentation is being uncovered, new suggestions are regularly being made. More at ease with archival sources than with the

monographs of younger scholars, Mr. Hilberg remains aloof from much
of this new work and new material. "Perpetrators Victims Bystanders"
reminds us of Mr. Hilberg's powerful, continuing presence. But now, for
students of the Holocaust, he seems less a pathfinder than a conscience.

Looking back four years later, Hilberg describes being shattered by
my review. The first chapter of his memoirs was called "The
Review," and in it he explored his emotional response to the words
I have just cited. He was deeply saddened. "So this is the end, the
real end, regardless of what may still happen," he pictured himself
as thinking. "That moment I was alone with myself, saying good-
bye to my life." Happily, that was not the end of the story. Courtly,
with something of an Old World Viennese courtesy, Hilberg could
be a gracious presence, and he certainly was to me. I met him at
conferences and meetings after what I have just described. At least
once we shared a meal together – I can't remember what we discussed, but while we avoided "the review," we talked about much
else. Is there a "lesson" here? All I can think of is that in the scholarly world we can only, all of us, do our best. In the end, someone
will do it better, and that is, in any work that is worthwhile, the
way it should be.

I once had a front row seat at a battle royal over Jewish testimony associated with an event, well known to the world of Holocaust
scholarship: the appearance of Daniel Jonah Goldhagen's *Hitler's
Willing Executioners*, a book that astoundingly became an international bestseller. I say astoundingly, because in the circles in which
I move there was barely a friendly word for this book, and historians to this day use it as a kind of foil for how not to interpret
perpetrators' motives on the killing of Jews. Denouncing what he
claimed was a historians' tendency to explain away the Germans'
participation in the Final Solution and to downplay their fanatic
hatred, Goldhagen claimed that Nazi Germany was driven by an
"eliminationist antisemitism" that governed practically the entire
German discourse on Jews.

The year 1989 saw the first meeting, at Northwestern University,
of "Lessons and Legacies," a large gathering of Holocaust specialists, continuing to meet biannually to communicate new scholarship

and spend time with each other and younger colleagues seeking to find secure employment. I recall chatting there with my friend Christopher Browning at a reception. Browning had presented a paper at that meeting, which appeared in *Ordinary Men*, a book he published a few years later and that quickly became a classic study of German perpetrators. In that work Browning described the murderous rampage, in territory taken from the Soviet Union, of a Hamburg-based reserve police battalion, as part of the shooting massacres of Jews in the East. Browning presented important new evidence arguing that the killers did not murder because of ideological zealotry, but rather because of relatively humdrum situational factors: conformity to the small group of which they were members, the brutalizing circumstances in which they operated, and with the help of various mechanisms of psychological adaptation. During the course of my conversation with Browning, an astonishingly young-looking man approached us, who I later learned was Daniel Goldhagen. "You scooped me," was what he said to Browning. We then had several meals together in the dining room of the Kellogg School of Business at Northwestern, thrashing out the issues between them.

Goldhagen seems to have emerged from these conversations with his views sharpened. In his *Hitler's Willing Executioners*, using overlapping evidence, he presented an analysis diametrically opposed to that of Browning. In Goldhagen's view, situational factors did not turn the shooters into killers; rather it was a special kind of German anti-Jewish ideology, which he called "eliminationist antisemitism." Goldhagen largely ignored Browning in his text, but conducted a take-no-prisoners guerrilla war against him in the dense underbrush of footnotes. Charging Browning with virtually every sin that a researcher could commit in misinterpreting evidence, he focused on one in particular – namely, that Browning had disparaged Jewish victims' accounts. In a later project, possibly as part of his response, Browning turned precisely to survivor testimony in an illuminating study of the Starachowice labour camps not far from Treblinka. Part of his achievement, Browning explained, was to show "how a historian of the Holocaust [can] use a variety of different, often conflicting and contradictory, in some cases clearly mistaken, memories of individual survivors as evidence to construct a history that otherwise, for lack of evidence, would not exist."

In a way, this dispute seems somewhat dated in 2015. No one would disagree that survivor testimony adds important dimensions to virtually any area one can think of in the study of the Holocaust. Certainly on a subject that treats the murder of European Jews, having recourse to such material not only makes sense but is a mark of respect that can hardly be ignored. However, it should be noted that many scholars, including Hilberg and Saul Friedländer, for example, distinguish between contemporary Jewish sources, which they find useful, and survivors' accounts, of which they are wary, because of the frailties of memory. But it is quite a leap to go from drawing upon Jewish accounts of particular incidents and circumstances to more general ruminations about what the Holocaust might teach us about human behaviour or the fate of the Jewish people. Not only are survivors' experiences inevitably limited to their own particular circumstances, but survivors are scarcely better placed than anyone else to assess the huge cultural, geographic, and temporal panorama of the Holocaust. Tellingly, survivors are notoriously unable to agree among themselves just what their experiences taught them, and what lessons might be drawn from what they endured. Moreover, they sometimes even disagree on whether they learned *anything at all* from their experiences.

A striking case in point is that of two of the most perceptive witnesses to emerge from the Holocaust, both of whom seem to have been consumed by their dreadful experiences in German camps and whose lives both ended tragically – likely by suicide in the case of the first, and certainly so in the second. The first is Primo Levi, the great Italian writer who suffered almost a year in Auschwitz and whose accounts carry unmistakable authority, and the second is the essayist Jean Améry, an Austrian Jew, born Hanns Chaim Mayer, who survived Auschwitz, Buchenwald, and Bergen Belsen, and whose meditations on his torture, which he describes unforgettably, are among the most arresting of his writings. A chemist by profession, and known for his spare, precise prose, Levi wrote of how much he learned in "the Lager," as he encapsulated his camp experience. "The Lager was a university," he wrote. "It taught us to look around and to measure men." Levi has much to say about what he learned, about how men adapt or fail to adapt, about what was the impact of their culture and learning, and what qualities of spirit might have preserved some from utter despair. Améry had a different opinion:

> We did not become wiser in Auschwitz, if by wisdom one understands positive knowledge of the world. We perceived nothing there that we would not already have been able to perceive on the outside; not a bit of it brought us practical guidance. In the camp, too, we did not become "deeper," if that calamitous depth is at all a definable intellectual quality. It goes without saying, I believe, that in Auschwitz we did not become better, more human, more humane, and more mature ethically. You do not observe dehumanized man committing his deeds and misdeeds without having all of your notions of inherent human dignity placed in doubt. We emerged from the camp stripped, robbed, emptied out, disoriented – and it was a long time before we were able even to learn the language of freedom.

This contrast may be repeated over and over again, with any number of writers. For Eli Wiesel, survivors bear witness; having experienced Auschwitz, he presents himself as a teacher, relaying something critical but ineffable – what he once called "the fall of mankind and the eclipse of the gods." But for Eli Pfefferkorn, who was at Majdanek, what he has to relay is terrifyingly banal: camp was mainstream, only at a terrible extreme. And so it goes for practically any pairing of Holocaust survivors on any number of issues one might think of. Survivors are often the first to debunk the authority of other survivors.

Survivors of the Holocaust sometimes become exceptionally anxious when they hear historians talk about episodes that they themselves lived. Such anxiety, notes the French historian Annette Wieviorka, represents a fear that is "not exclusive to survivors of the genocide: that of being dispossessed of one's history by someone outside the experience who claims to be telling it." At the same time, many are discomfited when people expect messages from them about the "meaning" of what they have endured. Aharon Appelfeld, one of Israel's foremost writers, is particularly insistent on refusing to extract lessons from his wartime Holocaust experiences. "The Holocaust belongs to the type of enormous experience which reduces one to silence. Any utterance, any statement, any 'answer' is tiny, meaningless and occasionally ridiculous," he once told Philip Roth. "Even the greatest of answers seems petty."

Among the most sensitive analysts of survivors' memories, Primo Levi challenged his own recollections of the past and warned others about how his and others' memories might be misshapen and misused for any number of purposes. "Human memory is a marvelous but fallacious instrument," he wrote in his last book, *The Drowned and the Saved*. "The memories that lie within us are not carved in stone; not only do they tend to become erased as the years go by, but often they change, or even grow, by incorporating extraneous features." Levi worried about how memory, when "evoked too often, and expressed in the form of a story, tends to become fixed in a stereotype, in a form tested by experience, crystallized, perfected, adorned, installing itself in the place of the raw memory and growing at its expense." Memory, he felt, had constantly to be tested, analysed, probed – something he did with his own memories, doubtless at great personal cost. The French historian Annie Kriegel, a highly assimilated Jew who escaped the Holocaust in France while engaged in the French Resistance, used to make this point vigorously when I knew her in the 1970s. She was adamant that experience did not give one credentials as an analyst of what had happened. "Just because you broke your leg," I heard her say irreverently, "does not make you an orthopedic surgeon." By this point in her life, I need to add, Kriegel was quite deaf. Even at the time, I wondered whether her insistence that survivors' claims might in good professional conscience be ignored might have come easier to her because she didn't hear them in the first place.

One of the things I learned when I travelled to Poland in the 1990s to work with colleagues on practical issues related to the camp of Auschwitz-Birkenau was how malleable Holocaust memories could be – firmly grounded on some points, but extremely susceptible to all kinds of influences and sometimes imperceptible changes on others. Even the language of communication mattered. Survivors interviewed in Yiddish responded quite differently from those who were interviewed in Polish. Most important of all when it came to general issues, I began to realize, was whether survivors had emigrated or had remained in Poland. Having grown up with Holocaust survivors in Toronto, I noticed differences between those whom I knew at home, others in Israel, and still others whom I met on visits to Europe. Researchers I knew had already tracked how notions of victimization varied according to emigration histories. The Polish psychologist and Holocaust researcher Barbara Engelking notes that Polish-Jewish emigrants to America

> found themselves after the war with all their baggage of experience and suffering in a country (I am thinking of Canada or the United States) whose society knew nothing of the realities of war. They knew about all its cruelty, the terror of occupation, the nightmare of the ghettos and camps only from newspapers and from second-hand sources. This must have made the behavior and problems of people from Europe all the more incomprehensible and sick to them. The new arrival from Europe did not "fit in to" the scale of values of American society, where satisfaction with life is ranked highly, along with not complaining and not revealing (except to an analyst) psychological or spiritual suffering. The survivors' problems could not be understood by a society that had not to the least degree shared their wartime experiences.

Unsurprisingly, survivors in the two postwar environments responded differently to their wartime past, and even more so when it came to issues touching the future, such as the lessons of the Holocaust. As interviewees, Polish survivors were extremely circumspect: testifying in a country where there was much hostility to Jews, and where the entire society had endured terrible oppression, they could be reluctant to single out their particularized victimization; those who went to America had other problems, often having to do with the perceived inability and unwillingness of their new country to contend with their pessimistic views about the depths to which humanity could sink; and those who moved to

Israel were frequently under great pressure to adapt their experiences to the Zionist narrative, one that had little interest in showcasing them as exemplars who had triumphed over adversity. To colleagues in this field such as Engelking, the psychologist, such things were obvious. To me they were a revelation.

Interviewers' expectations, as survey experts know well, affect responses of interviewees. And so the considerable attention given to lessons of the Holocaust in our culture has had the effect, over time, of eliciting from survivors all kinds of admonitions that, left to their own devices, they might have been hesitant to offer. We need to remember that Holocaust survivors, especially those in Communist Poland, frequently found extraordinary – and perhaps somewhat suspicious – the whole experience of being questioned about their wartime ordeal. What use would be made of their responses? Could the interviewers be trusted? What was the point of it all? One Polish researcher, Joachim Schwartz, commented on how interviews pushed the subjects to articulate "the moral of the story," in other words, "the lessons of the Holocaust." Here he is, following the logic of many of his interviewees:

> The ends of all stories irrespective of whether they are fairy tales or descriptions of certain events, usually have a moral, a point, a lesson, which is why the story was told and which is to be communicated to the audience, which is designed to stimulate the audience to thought. A moral of this kind only achieves its intended goal if the story, event, recounted has a beginning and an end: it is only then that you can comprehend it and evaluate it.

To make sense of their accounts, in other words, interviewees seek to put them into some wider framework or context. And so encouraging survivors to speak about the Holocaust encourages them to provide lessons. Alternatively, standing back from this process and abandoning the challenge of providing "meaning" to terrible events becomes increasingly difficult.

Scrupulously modest on this and other subjects, Primo Levi constantly faced people who wanted him to define lessons. Here is his commentary on his short-lived experience as a speaker in classrooms. Exhausted by his efforts to be forthcoming, he expressed his frustration: "one of the questions that gets repeated and repeated is the question of why it happened, why there are wars, why the camps were built, why the Jews were exterminated, and it is a question to which I have no answer. No one does. Why there are wars, why was the First World War and the Second World War ... is a question that torments me because I have no answer."

Levi, of course, spoke only for himself. But having done a fair amount of public speaking in schools on the subject, I have plenty of sympathy with his sense of helplessness. And admiration, too, for Levi was forthright in saying that he *just didn't know* – something which I particularly admire him for confessing. Too many, I believe, both survivors and especially so-called "experts," cannot resist the temptation to invoke the Holocaust to make some general point or another, on which their opinion is no better grounded than anyone else's.

Everyone who attends even an occasional lecture on the Holocaust will have witnessed times when the question period explodes into anger because of a survivor's objections to something that was said. These are painful moments, and many seek to avoid them at almost all costs. "The suffering conveyed by the story of a survivor," writes Annette Wieviorka, "by one who may be the last repository of a procession of the dead whose memory he carries with him – paralyzes the historian." Historians know about frailties of memory. And they also know how much the facts of survival can be interwoven with feelings of guilt, inadequacy, and shame – sentiments against which victims sometimes push back violently, brandishing their victimhood as a certificate of authority. But it is hard, in a contest that sometimes cannot be avoided, sometimes very hard, to assert a counter-authority to that of memory, namely the claims of reason and evidence.

Among the lessons of the Holocaust heard by Jewish audiences, many entail a generous salute to survivors who endured so much at one part of their lives and who somehow managed to emerge from the horror with a positive message. These lessons involve claims about hope, human resilience, or the triumph of the human spirit. Perhaps the most common of these is the notion that survival in itself constitutes a lesson – the capacity of Jews to endure the harshest oppression and to emerge from it with their spirit intact and with optimism for the future. During the 1970s and 1980s, partially in response to the argument made by Raul Hilberg about Jewish passivity in the face of persecution, historians presented a case for Jewish agency, often summarized by the Hebrew term *amidah*, or "standing up against," using a vocabulary summarized by Christopher Browning with the terms "ingenuity, resourcefulness, adaptability, perseverance and endurance." Such claims cannot help but generate adherents, for after all the alternative, the possibility that there is nothing positive that Jews can take from the Holocaust, would almost certainly leave them with an even greater sense of emptiness and futility than is already associated with the Jewish catastrophe.

A moment's reflection, however, should suggest how problematic is this idea of a Jewish triumph over great odds as a lesson of the Holocaust. My colleague Doris Bergen points out how hungry is popular culture for a redemptive part of the story – practically anything that might provide a silver lining to meaningless misery and unmitigated barbarism. Whether with Holocaust literature or Holocaust monuments or Holocaust commemorations or even Holocaust history, there is a constant tug towards a redemptive message. And yet notwithstanding this aspiration, historical investigation suggests that whatever intervened in the processes of mass murder to save the lives of a few cannot be the stuff of unqualified collective celebration. As every historian knows, to survive was to benefit from extraordinary luck. Chance, more than anything else, determined that a tiny remnant would escape the machinery of destruction. That is what occasioned a moment's peace, a crust of bread, a guard's inattention, or an opportunity to speak the right language at the right moment. Moreover, it would be wrong to assume that, under Nazism, a life force commonly persisted. In rare circumstances it did, and we may rejoice in the instances have been recorded in ghetto diaries and in memories of the tiny remnant that managed to endure. But the opposite was sadly far too common – a point recently made by a Holocaust scholar, Amos Goldberg of the Hebrew University, in a careful study of Holocaust diaries. In evidence, I submit the terrible *Warsaw Diary* entry of Chaim Kaplan, for May 18, 1941: "without knowing it we accept the Torah of the Nazis and follow its path. Nazism has conquered our entire world."

In my experience, survivors know these grim realities best, and none have articulated with more clarity the effects of trauma that crushed the life out of so many victims before they perished. Henry Friedlander, both a survivor of Auschwitz and a distinguished Holocaust historian, loathed the very term "survivor" and refused to accept it in his own case. His reason was precisely the serendipity of his own escape from death, for which he felt he deserved no special recognition. It seems hardly reasonable, in my view, to award the tiny numbers who somehow managed to escape the worst a badge of Jewish achievement. Nor does it seem right to privilege the few who "did not give in to despair" over the many who sank beneath the weight of despondency and pain. Indeed, whatever personal qualities may have played a role in individuals' managing to escape the fate the Germans had in mind, in collective terms the successful application of such resources hardly seems to be a fair or just cause for individual distinction. That is why many survivors feel embarrassed at how readily the public at large not only celebrates their survival but identifies as exemplary personal qualities deemed to have made the decisive contributions to this outcome.

This assessment has put me at odds with people of good will who have proposed to "honour the survivors" with dinners, tributes, and other distinctions. I understand the generous impulses that usually lie behind such exercises – an urge to try to close the gap, if only just a little, between those who suffered great torments at one part of their lives, and possibly in the years that have followed, and those who did not; but at the end of the day it seems to me that, along with their invidious distinctions, these gestures misshape an important part of Holocaust history. The gaps cannot in the end be closed. Those who perished should not be honoured for things they did not do. And those who survived are not necessarily exemplars. While Jewish agency undoubtedly existed, those who were victimized and who survived were not generally heroes, to whom medals are awarded, but ordinary people like the rest of us, and like those who perished, with their share of strengths and frailties. Survivors whom I know appreciate these things and are prepared to leave it at that.

Closely associated with lessons about survival are claims that the Holocaust teaches fidelity to Jewish peoplehood and the perils of Jewish assimilation in the face of antisemitism. Margaret MacMillan notes how common it is to use history to promote group solidarity, and to this I would add that the invigoration of communal identities can be a response of battered minorities who look back with anguish on their victimization and wonder how they might have avoided the worst. Interest in the solidarity of victims was certainly evident when I first studied Jewish matters in the 1960s, deriving importantly, in my case and that of many of my peers, from the identity politics of African Americans in the United States. Fidelity, in that context, meant not "selling out," "keeping the faith," and maintaining one's "authenticity." Attuned to these signals, I was part of a generation of historians who explored the theme of Jewish assimilation, particularly in France and Germany during a time of resurgent antisemitism in the 1930s, and did so as part of their reflection on the Holocaust that followed.

On this issue as on so many others, Hannah Arendt spoke to me and many of my contemporaries in the 1960s – in part, of course, because as a refugee from Nazism she was *there* at the time, as well as because she spoke so boldly about matters of identity politics. What was particularly attractive about Arendt to some, including me, was the way that she combined a promotion of Jewish universalism with a forceful expression of Jewish identity. I do not recall knowing about her boldly beginning a lecture in Cologne less than a decade after the end of the war with the words, "I am a German Jew driven from my homeland," but had I done so I would certainly have admired the turn of phrase and the sentiment behind it. I drew upon her writings when I argued in my work on French Jews at the time of the Dreyfus Affair that their dilution of

Jewish identity weakened communal solidarity. Putting Jewish assimilation in the context of the rise of antisemitism in Europe in the
1890s, Arendt insisted that the Jews' efforts to abandon Jewishness
and assume the identities of their non-Jewish neighbours were not
only bound to fail but actually stimulated hatred and racism. Her
argument was difficult to follow – and I later came to think that
she went off the analytical rails when she made these points. At the
time, however, she persuaded me that assimilation obscured warning signs for Jews and diminished their capacity to predict how
dangerous was the situation that they faced in many countries.

I should add that, preoccupied with Arendt as my contemporaries and I certainly were, we were largely unaware of the seriousness of her liaison with her professor at Marburg and future Nazi,
the philosopher Martin Heidegger. Theirs was a passionate affair
that began in 1925, when he was thirty-five and she was eighteen;
the affair continued for several years until she went into exile in
France, and involved a famous and protracted postwar reconcilia-
tion in a friendship that continued to her death in 1975. There has
been endless thought, writing, chatter, and representation in film
and theatre about this relationship. What really brought it into the
public arena was the publication of letters between the two by the
novelist and biographer Elzbieta Ettinger, in 1995. I can only wonder about what might have been the effect on Arendt's admirers
had this material come to light thirty years before.

Entirely different from the perspective of Hannah Arendt is the
insistence upon fidelity to Jewish tradition and identity as a moral or spiritual lesson – a claim powerfully articulated in the late
1960s by Emil Fackenheim as the 614th commandment for Jews,
described in the last chapter. This response might more properly
be considered a religious obligation rather than a history lesson,
a call for commitment to the maintenance of Jewish life and identity as supreme values in their own right. Extreme versions of this
commitment have prompted some Orthodox groups to identify
Jewish assimilation as a "silent Holocaust" that is working, as did
that of Hitler, to achieve the end of the Jewish people. There are
also staunch spokesmen for Orthodoxy who see the Holocaust
as God's punishment for Zionism or the liberalization of Jewish

practice. Historians generally consider themselves outside these debates – and justifiably relieved for being so. But they can hardly escape contributing to a discussion that crucially involves historical facts. In this case, historians know that the Germans and most of their henchmen in Nazi-occupied Europe had no interest in distinguishing between assimilated and unassimilated Jews, between those who had well-developed Jewish identities and those who did not, and indeed Hitler's Jewish experts worked assiduously to collapse such distinctions, doing their best to see that persecution and eventually mass murder were extended even to those with the most remote connection to Jewishness. Moreover, to stigmatize Jews who chose a weakening of their Jewish practice or identity would be to participate in the logic of Nazi thinking in which communal identities are essentialist categories, unaffected by individual choices or preferences. From my perspective, it is hard to believe that anyone could take such views seriously as a lesson of the Holocaust.

On this point I would only add that, as with so many other issues, Holocaust survivors have taken radically different positions on matters of Jewish commitment. As we know, many Jews who survived the Holocaust sought for any number of reasons to disguise, ignore, or even reject their Jewish backgrounds. Indeed, the range of Jewish responses to the Holocaust extends across the whole spectrum on matters of identity, willingness to recount Holocaust experiences, and wider conclusions from either of these. For reasons having to do with the difficulties in investigating such elusive issues as well as clarifying suppressed identities, there is little research on this subject and little reference to the matter in discussions of lessons. Moreover, just as such Jewish responses differ across national, cultural, and other categories, they also shift over time and across generations. Poland, home to over three million Jews before the war, most of whom were murdered or later fled attacks on Jews by the Communist regime in 1968, again provides a case in point. Thousands of Poles are now claiming, or reclaiming, a Jewish identity – for which there is invariably some story of escape from the Holocaust during the war years. Many have discovered their Jewish backgrounds only as adults, from aging parents or other family members. These are, as my friend Rabbi Dow Marmur has put it, "Jews by Surprise." What is so interesting is the eagerness of many Poles to embrace their Jewish heritage, rather than to continue to hide it.

No account of lessons intended for Jews could ignore the March of the Living, described on its Facebook page as "an international educational program bringing Jewish teens to Poland on Holocaust Remembrance day and to Israel to learn the lessons of the Holocaust and to lead the Jewish people into the future vowing NEVER AGAIN." Established in 1988 with funding from the Conference on Jewish Material Claims against Germany, the March is a kind of pilgrimage in which Jewish adolescents from various countries go first to Poland, to visit Holocaust-related sites, including death camps such as Auschwitz and Treblinka, and then on to Israel, where they celebrate Yom Ha'atzmaut (Israel's Independence Day). Since its inception, as many as 150,000 young people have gone on these trips. Photographs of participants graphically illustrate their act of collective redemption: draped in Israeli flags and with banners held high, marchers parade into the death camps and other sites in Poland, and are shown in expressions of grief and joyous group solidarity. An emotionally draining experience about which there have been varying reactions, both highly critical and full of praise, the March of the Living has been a platform for communicating lessons with regard to both the Holocaust and its link to present-day Zionist commitment.

Particularly in its early years, the March of the Living was the object of important criticisms: that it presented both Poland and Israel in highly stereotyped perspectives, the former as a benighted country soaked in antisemitism, and the latter as a land without blemish that was the embodiment of Jewish life-affirmation after the decimations of the Holocaust; and that the organizers employed sleep deprivation and other techniques to instil predetermined messages rather than encouraging the young people to think for themselves. No doubt they were susceptible. "There's nothing like a few days in eastern Europe to bring out the Jew in you," comments the Israeli humorist and short-story writer Etgar Keret. Right-wing religious Zionists, seeing in the March a competition for young Jewish hearts and minds, levelled a barrage of criticism

against the March of the Living after a decade and a half of operation, claiming that it had no educational value and that money expended on such trips could be better spent in study of the Torah.
Twenty-five years after its foundation, the March continues, somewhat battered by financial irregularities associated with one of its
founders, a former Israeli finance minister, Avraham Hirschson,
convicted of embezzlement by a Tel Aviv court in 2009, but with
reported improvements in the manner in which the intended
"messages" are communicated in both Poland and Israel. However
evaluated, I think it fair to say that the March represents a major
community commitment to the lessons of the Holocaust as we have
understood them here, operating on a global plane, and with significant communal commitment both in Israel and the Diaspora.

Perhaps the most frequently articulated lesson of the Holocaust
expressed by Jews is about power. "When living among wolves
one must act like a wolf or be eaten," one interviewee explained
recently. Intended as a *Jewish* lesson, that is, intended to speak to
Jews, the message here is not about any particular virtue associated with the exercise of power or any celebration of power as a
positive attribute, but rather about power as a means of survival.
"One of the lessons of the Holocaust is that any minority group,
and especially the Jews, must protect itself against the potential
for destruction and massacre by a hostile majority," this commentator continued. "The lesson of Jewish history is that safety
is only to be found with a Jewish army in a Jewish state," wrote
Israeli prime minister Benjamin Netanyahu in his 1993 book, *A
Place among the Nations*:

> if there had been an Israel earlier in this century, there surely would have
> been no Holocaust. There would have been a country willing to take the
> Jewish refugees when America, Britain, and the other nations refused.
> There would have been an army ready to fight for them. If the past was
> lacking in this regard, the future is not: The Jews are no longer helpless,
> no longer lacking the capacities to assert their case and to fight for it.
> It is an incontestable fact that the establishment of the Jewish state has

retrieved for the Jews the ability to again seize their destiny, to again control their fate.

The problem, continued Netanyahu, and in this he echoed much of the thinking of the Israeli and the Zionist Right, was that Jews needed to accommodate themselves to a new reality of Jewish power; instead of doing so, they continued to suffer from "apolitical habits of thought and behavior acquired in years of exile." Ruth Wisse, a former Montrealer and distinguished professor of Yiddish literature at Harvard, has a much more intricate view about Jewish power, its inflections over time, and its interactions with the history of Zionism. Nevertheless, she sees power as the key lesson of the Holocaust, which (and I take some small liberty here with her discourse, although I don't think much) "those who aspire to be decent human beings would be morally obtuse to the point of wickedness" to ignore. Wisse's point is that Jews are particularly prone to naiveté on the issue of power. Over long years of experience, they seem to have been especially inhibited "from understanding their political interaction with other nations." In a recent column, the Israeli journalist Arik Elman put the matter succinctly: "Jews must be united, Jews must be armed, Jews must achieve and preserve national sovereignty."

Knowing his interest in the subject of the wartime Yishuv, or Jewish community in Palestine, not to mention the fact that he had been there at the time, I put this issue to Yehuda Bauer when I was a visitor at the Hebrew University's Institute for Advanced Studies some thirty-five years ago. As so often, Bauer was sceptical of received wisdom – even, as in this case, when such wisdom was a core doctrine of Israel's Zionist establishment. He spoke with authority as a former member of the Palmach, the elite fighting force of the Haganah, the army of the Yishuv, and also of Mapam, a left-wing partner of the Israeli Labour Party. Born in Prague in 1926 and emigrating to Palestine via Poland and Romania with his family in 1939, he became Israel's leading historian of the Holocaust. I recall his particularly broad command of Holocaust issues in general and the Yishuv in particular, the latter widely appreciated outside the country because of a 1970 English translation of his book, *From Diplomacy to Resistance: A History of Jewish Palestine*. What follows is the example that Bauer raised for my own and my fellow participants' consideration in our Holocaust seminar at the Hebrew University.

Bauer described the Yishuv in 1942, when Palestinian Jews had incomplete but nevertheless credible information about mass murder that raged in the East. As we now know, there were horrific shootings of nearly a million Jews in territory captured from the Soviets by the Germans following the June 1941 Barbarossa invasion of the Soviet Union; extensive clearances of ghettos to which tens of thousands of Jews had been dispatched from Western and Central Europe prior to their deportations to killing sites in Poland; and finally, the inauguration and evolution of facilities for the murder, using poison gas, of hundreds of thousands of helpless Jews, rounded up from across Europe and deported to the East. At that time, the Yishuv was home to some five hundred thousand Jews, about a third of the population of Mandatory Palestine. To defend itself, this population depended upon an apparently outclassed British army in the North African desert, pressed against the gates of Egypt by Erwin Rommel's Afrika Korps. With the British seemingly on the edge of collapse, the situation seemed desperate. Half a million Jews were at risk of massacre.

Thanks to the work of German historians Klaus-Michael Mallmann and Martin Cüppers, we now know about the Germans' murderous intentions for Jewish Palestine in 1942. That summer the Afrika Korps was ready to capture Cairo and the Suez Canal and then proceed to Palestine, sweeping the British before them. Along with the mechanized German forces and infantry was an SS Einsatzkommando unit headed by SS-Obersturmbannführer Walter Rauch, an experienced Nazi administrator and "one of those most centrally responsible for the mass murder of the Jews" in the East. Rauch himself was intimately acquainted with the operation of mobile killing units from his service in Serbia and occupied Soviet territory. His newly organized unit, while small, was nevertheless expected to deploy whatever Arab collaborators would be necessary – and in the minds of the German planners, at least, such adherence was not expected to pose any special difficulties. At the beginning of the summer of 1942 all seemed to go well for the Germans. Rommel's forces captured the deep sea port of Tobruk and later the fortress of Mersa Matruh. The road appeared open to Egypt and beyond. This was, say our authors, the starting point for bringing the Holocaust to the Jewish national home. Throughout the Yishuv, it was widely feared that the Germans would break through. But unexpectedly, the tide turned. In July, British forces stalled the German advance eastwards in the First Battle of El Alamein. And then, as a result of heavy fighting in October and November, the British Eighth Army under General Bernard Montgomery broke through the German lines at El Alamein, forced the Panzers all the way back to Tunisia, and turned the tide in North Africa. Egypt remained in Allied hands, as did Palestine, and thus the Yishuv was saved.

The massacre that was so feared by the Jews had not been a figment of their imaginations, however. Historians have described the plans that Jewish leaders grimly devised in the event of a German breakthrough: the defenders' idea was to harass the invaders even while retreating northwards, to pull the Jewish population away from the expected German invasion, evacuating as many as possible, and to organize a last ditch stand on the slopes of Mount Carmel, overlooking Haifa. Yitzhak Tabenkin, a charismatic leader of the kibbutz movement and an associate of David Ben Gurion, echoed the near despair of the Jewish leadership: "Our feeling is that of ultimate loneliness … There is no way to know how many Jews will remain alive … There is no guarantee that the Nazis will not exterminate the entire one hundred percent … Bitter is the knowledge of our solitude and the knowledge that the world is our enemy."

The sixteen-year-old Yehuda Bauer and his father, both mobilized for battle, were ready for the Germans. Yehuda recalled his father, who had served as an officer in the First World War and had fought against the Italians, saying that he would not be taken alive. Mallmann and Cüppers assess the situation:

> all the defense plans and all the speculation about them indicate that
> the Yishuv would hardly have been in a position to organize a mass

evacuation in time and provide sufficient opposition to the *Afrika Korps* and its Arab allies. On a larger scale but otherwise analogous to the armed Jewish resistance in Europe, there would have been a desperate battle against the Axis and its Arab allies in Palestine. In the end, the Yishuv would undoubtedly have been completely annihilated. The Jews of Palestine were saved only by the military developments on the North African front.

What does this example tell us? Most importantly, it suggests some of the hazards of counterfactual history. Yes, it is possible that had there been a Jewish state in Palestine in 1942 the Jews might have stopped Rommel and the Afrika Korps. Yes, the Jews there might have escaped what the Germans had in mind for them. But probably not. Much more likely the Jewish state would have turned out to be a deadly trap for the Jews. Had it not been for the outcome of the Second Battle of El Alamein, the Germans probably would have destroyed whatever the Jews had achieved in Palestine and murdered most of the Jewish population there. And by the same token, had more Jews been allowed to escape to Palestine in the 1930s, even more might have been caught by the Wehrmacht in 1942. Speculation can generate any number of scenarios. But speculative scenarios generate unreliable lessons. Meanwhile, confronted with opposing possibilities, most historians yield the field to the speculators and the politicians. Historians have enough trouble with what *did* happen, most of them will say, without speculating on what might have happened.

The most recent pursuit of might-have-beens is a persistent campaign in the United States to stigmatize the American president Franklin D. Roosevelt, at the time of the Holocaust fervently admired by most American Jews for the Jewish appointments to his administration, his liberalism, and his determination to pursue the conflict with Nazi Germany. Critics now charge the American president with not having done enough to assist Jewish refugees in the 1930s and with failing to mount a rescue campaign during the Holocaust itself. And along with this cause, campaigners have focused admiration and praise on the right-wing Zionist activist Hillel Kook, nephew of the first chief rabbi of Palestine and known by his *nom de guerre* as Peter Bergson. Bergson constantly fought to get the Americans to do more. While historians are certainly aware of Roosevelt's shortcomings and sometimes devious evasions, they also point to the president's political challenges from those with different priorities and his concerns to prosecute the war against the Germans without hindrance from any quarter.

Most writers have tried to find a balanced view. But a significant body of opinion, led by American historian Rafael Medoff, the founding director of the David Wyman Institute for Holocaust Studies, named after the American author of *The Abandonment of the Jews*, vocally dissents. According to its website, the Wyman Institute "focuses on the abandonment of Europe's Jews during the Nazi era, the efforts to promote rescue, and the moral and historical lessons of those experiences." The organization's recent eleventh national conference was titled "75 Years since the 'Voyage of the Damned'" (a reference to the turning back to Europe of Jewish refugees from Germany aboard the *SS St Louis* in 1939) and subtitled provocatively with a question, "Are We Doomed to Repeat It?" Medoff has fired off a constant barrage of arguments on this subject and refuses to give any quarter. Many think his views not only blinkered by excessive hindsight but also politically tinged by support from the Israeli and American Right and linked to a sense that some Jews have of being constantly under siege, especially over Israel. Bergson's group in the United States, representatives of the right-wing Revisionist opponents of Labour Zionism, are part of the political family whose descendants are the modern-day Likud in Israel. Their "not-so-subtle message," writes Laurence Zuckerman in the *Nation*, is that "like the Jews of Europe in 1939, Israel is under an existential threat and cannot count on anyone for help – even the United States, even liberals, even Jews in the United States, most of whom are insufficiently committed to Zionism. A sell-out happened before, and no matter how friendly a president or a country may appear to be, it can happen again." The lesson is betrayal – first by Roosevelt, no friend of the Jews, and then by the historians, who have failed and continue to fail to draw the obvious lessons. The Jews are alone. One should perhaps add that in the view of many, this way of looking at things runs the risk of becoming a self-fulfilling prophecy.

The most common of the many lessons of the Holocaust for Jews concerns repetition. Signalled by the slogan "Never again!" the fear lurks that in some manner the Holocaust could repeat itself. Questions about this persist, and those who claim expertise are constantly asked for their evaluation. Are the latest outrages against Jews a portent? Is Israel, the collective Jew, doomed to suffer from a "new antisemitism"? Why is the world so blind to these realities? A majority of Americans actually believe a recurrence of the Holocaust against Jews in Europe is possible, according to a survey sponsored by a group called the Committee of Concerned Christians ten years ago. "Unless a full-scale program is implemented to prevent another Holocaust, a more accurate slogan is 'It will happen again,'" said Ben Friedman, the founder and spokesman of the committee. Nearly half of Israelis believe that the Holocaust could happen again, reported the left-of-centre *Haaretz* recently. The late Robert Wistrich, who headed an institute for the study of antisemitism at the Hebrew University and who wrote a very long book on the subject, suggested this as well. "We are in an era once again where the Jews are facing genocidal threats as a people," he told one interviewer. "We have not been in that situation for quite a while. And maybe this is the first time since the Shoah that [Jews] feel that this is palpable." To be sure, Wistrich acknowledged, Jews made similar predictions after Israel's wars in 1967 and 1973. "Yet the current threat is much more serious," he insisted: "There are people who seek the Jews' extinction and aren't shy about their intentions." Wistrich was careful to hedge his commentary. However, the widely repeated headline for his interview was entitled "The Holocaust Can Happen Again, Warns Top Anti-Semitism Scholar."

When beamed specifically at Jews, this message arouses deep apprehensions about the propagation of universal messages about the Holocaust. "The Holocaust was not an interfaith experience," warns Walter Reich, a former director of the United States Holocaust Memorial Museum. Reich laments the growing effort to universalize the Holocaust, "to make it into a lesson about 'man's inhumanity to man.'" Such efforts, he and others feel, are part of an effort to distract attention from the very real threats Jews face. One current of critical analysis of Holocaust themes sees great danger in the "dejudaization" of the murder of European Jews, obscuring the Jewish identities of the victims and blocking out the specifically anti-Jewish objectives of the perpetrators – "stealing the Holocaust," as one writer put it. A related threat, in the view of an admittedly small minority, is what they see as a perverse tendency to dwell upon the positive lessons that derive from rescuers of Jews. An "orgy of Pollyannaism" is the harsh view of an American academic, Edward Alexander. The iconic example of this process is the *Diary of Anne Frank*, still the most widely read book on the Holocaust globally, and famous for its humanistic message of a better world – especially Anne's closing comment from an acclaimed Broadway play of 1955 in which Anne was made to say, "In spite of everything, I still believe that people are really good at heart," which misshapes her original meaning and take her words out of their July 1944 context. Not only does this rendering of Anne Frank do violence to her meaning at the time, its most vociferous critics say, but also it is part of a longstanding, concerted effort to ignore or downplay the lethal, global hatred of Jews. In the periodical of an organization called Americans for a Safe Israel, columnist Daniel Greenfield denounces the "humanist hijackers of the Holocaust." "The Holocaust [has] a very important lesson to teach both Jews and non-Jews," he writes. "Not the lesson of universal tolerance, but the lesson of the need for individuals and communities to be able to defend themselves." Darkly pessimistic about human nature, this perspective laments using the Holocaust to promote tolerance or universal brotherhood. Naive views such as these thrived after the Second World War, Greenfield says. But it's over. Genocide persists. International organizations are corrupt. Islamic fundamentalism promotes a new antisemitism. Jews are as threatened as ever. Israel is at perilous risk. "The great humanistic experiment is dead, though its stench is impossible to escape."

These are extreme views. But much more common is the identification of important moments of Holocaust history and the proclamation that what is happening in the world today is "just like," or "reminiscent of," or "analogous to," key landmarks on the road to the Holocaust. In these constructs, the lesson is to see the world through the histories of Nazism and the Second World War. While there are many versions of this trope, probably the most commonly articulated involve references to the year 1938, a key moment on the historical path to the Holocaust, as historians generally agree. This was a year of Nazism's significant tightening its grip on Germany; an increasingly ferocious assault on the Jewish population and the *Kristallnacht* pogrom across Germany; the *Anschluss*, or absorption into Nazi Germany of Austria, and the extension of the persecution of Jews to that country; the striking failure of liberal democracies to respond positively to an accelerating flow of refugees, especially with the Evian Conference; the crisis over Czechoslovakia, the Munich conference, and increasingly evident German preparations for aggression; and a radically worsening situation for Jews in many other countries with large Jewish populations, most particularly Poland, Romania, and Hungary. This was what one German document programmatically identified as "the fateful year" of the Nazis' assault on Jews, and there are some who even consider these events as the beginning of the Holocaust.

Signalling alarm, numerous commentators now read the threats to Jews as akin to those of 1938 – particularly with reference to antisemitic events in Europe, or threats to Israel coming from a nuclear-armed Iran, or a tide of isolationism identified with the Obama administration in United States. In 2006, Israeli prime minister Benjamin Netanyahu pointedly drew an analogy between Iran and Nazi Germany in a speech to the annual United Jewish Communities General Assembly in Los Angeles. "It's 1938 and Iran is Germany," he said at the time, repeating the line several times in his speech. "No one will defend the Jews if the Jews don't defend themselves," he added. Netanyahu's minister of defence, Ehud Barak, a member of the Labour Party, took a similarly menacing posture towards Iran. In 2007, the Center for Jewish Studies of Queens College in New York City hosted an entire conference on this subject. "Since 1945 I was not as afraid as I am now," said Nobel laureate and Holocaust survivor Elie Wiesel, introducing a film on antisemitism in 2012. "Can the brainwashed learn the lessons of the Holocaust in time?" asks the title of a recent blog by Phyllis Chesler, a popular, self-described radical feminist, psychotherapist, and commentator on Jewish issues. The message is clearly one of Jewish vulnerability, and even if not explicitly predicting a Holocaust, the understanding is of a catastrophically dangerous situation for Jews or the Jewish state. Failing to see things this way is almost invariably branded "appeasement," with an obvious analogy to British Prime Minister Neville Chamberlain and his government. And accompanying this message, one might add, is the inference that such a situation might well be, as historians sometimes think was the case with 1938, the very last chance to stop a menacing juggernaut.

Yet even when it is articulated as a lesson of the Holocaust, with all the emotion and authority that entails, many Israelis reject the analogy. At the highest level of Israel's strategic planning, military and intelligence chiefs have taken a different view. "While the prime minister and the minister of defense thought their subordinates lacked historical perspective and courage," writes journalist Ari Shavit in his recent book, *My Promised Land*, "the top army intelligence brass thought of their superiors as messianic, warmongering zealots. The fierce struggle between the two groups became personal, visceral, and ugly." As the debate intensified, so did explicit criticisms of the 1938 analogy. Commentators added that even in Europe Jews are not helpless victims, that many other groups feel equally if not more threatened, often with good reason, that Israel is hardly a powerless actor in the Middle East, that there are countervailing forces everywhere, and so on. "Can everyone please take a deep breath?" recommended television journalist Fareed Zakaria in a column on this subject some years ago.

No doubt, however, the Holocaust is a potent argument and strikes a deep chord among Jews both in Israel and elsewhere. The reluctance to see the gravity of the situation is itself seen as something history warns against, say those with the 1930s and 1940s constantly in mind. Jews prefer to hide harsh realities this way, say others. Going further, they often attribute Jews' unwillingness to accept the most alarming scenario to their desperation to fit in, to hide their Jewish identities by not rocking the boat. And at the most extreme there is the accusation of Jewish self-hatred – an explanation for Jewish behaviour that has prompted both public accusations of fecklessness and even university courses in the subject. As with 1938, goes the argument, excessively optimistic perspectives or illusions of peacemaking or a constant preference for diplomacy are familiar illusions, and stigmatizing such views is presented as something history teaches us to do. And finally, a reliance on countervailing forces – whether the United States, liberal democracies, or geopolitical complexities, among other factors – is scorned or derided with reference to history. "Jews believed such things in 1938, and see where that got them," it is said. "That is the lesson of history."

chapter five

Israeli Lessons

Yad Vashem, Israel's commemorative and research institution for the Holocaust, or Shoah as it is known in Hebrew, is a place of paradox. A national memorial, it calls to mind the greatest of horrors; but it is a peaceful place, often sun-drenched, blending into a carefully landscaped mountaintop that seems about as far from sites of mass murder as one could imagine. Built on forty-five acres atop a ridge on the western hills of Jerusalem, more than 2,500 feet above sea level and with spectacular views of the valley below, Yad Vashem is a major cluster of buildings, the size of a small university campus, much of it built or clad in a creamy white or gold-coloured Jerusalem stone and including imposing memorials, an impressive and newly renovated museum, an art museum, synagogue, decorative garden, administrative and academic offices, and places for public gatherings of all sorts, plus quiet walkways that link one place to another. Its postal address is Har Hazikaron, the Hill of Remembrance. Some fifteen acres have been set aside for distinctive landscaping, and stones and trees commemorating those the institution designates the Righteous among the Nations – gentiles who helped protect Jews from their oppressors during the Holocaust. Its name is taken from a verse in the Book of Isaiah, "Even unto them will I give in mine house and within my walls *a place and a name* [in Hebrew, *yad vashem*] better than of sons and of daughters: I will give them an everlasting name, that shall not be cut off," conveying the idea of a repository of memories of the nameless victims of the Holocaust. When Yad Vashem was established as the Martyrs' and Heroes' Remembrance Authority in 1953 by a law of the Israeli parliament, or Knesset, the statute solemnly defined its mandate as being "to establish memorial projects at its own initiative and under its own management, to gather, study and publish testimony about the Holocaust; and to impart its lessons to the people." Lessons, then, were there at the institution's creation, as much a part of the institution as its Jerusalem stone.

Today, Yad Vashem is understood to be at the heart of Israel's self-definition. As a matter of course, distinguished visitors from abroad come there soon after they arrive in the country – just as they were once taken, in the early days of the Jewish state, to visit a kibbutz or some other modern-day achievement of which the country was rightfully proud. Speeches of welcome and visitors' reactions have hardened into a standard pattern. As the Israeli intellectual Bernard Avishai puts it, these orations "must include a syllogism in which the 'Holocaust' forms the first part and 'the Jewish state' the second." What is being intoned, sometimes explicitly, are oft-alluded-to lessons.

Tellingly, there has never been a consensus about how these should be understood. The earliest Holocaust researchers associated with Yad Vashem were clearly divided over priorities and directions. As charted by an Israeli scholar, Boaz Cohen, some survivor-intellectuals, mainly from Poland and Lithuania, looked far afield for implications, posing big questions concerning the nature of the Jewish catastrophe for the Jewish people and the European civilization of which they had been a part. Their starting point, Cohen notes, was "the concept of the people as an organic entity with its own existence, and an emphasis on social aspects." Those who came from the young Israeli academic world centred on the Hebrew University of Jerusalem, however, drawing on German historical traditions, took a much more scholarly approach and sought to integrate the Holocaust into the great stream of Jewish history written by historians. Emphases differed. But as the debates persisted, one thing was clear: for both groups, Holocaust wounds were fresh and seeped into each interpretation.

A quest for deeper significance that mingled with the mourning process was therefore unavoidable. Moreover, it was practically impossible for these pioneers of Holocaust inquiry to separate the study of what the Jews had been through from the reality of a new and still beleaguered Jewish state fresh from its War of Independence and from the Zionist world view that was so actively shaping the national ethos. It is not by accident that Yad Vashem is adjacent to Israel's main military cemetery. Nearby is the tomb of Theodore Herzl, the founder of political Zionism, and a memorial to Jewish civilian victims of terrorist attacks going back to 1851. To the formidable Ben-Zion Dinur, Zionist, politician, and Hebrew University historian, Israeli minister of education from 1951 to 1955 and the first chairman of Yad Vashem, the Holocaust reinforced the centrality of Israel for the Jewish people. "The fundamental lesson of the Holocaust," declared Dinur, is that "the Diaspora is not only a disaster and a catastrophe, but also a sin and a transgression: 'Diaspora' and 'destruction' are not two separate categories; rather, 'Diaspora' includes 'destruction.'" It was for Yad Vashem, its founders agreed, to conduct the research necessary to clarify these lessons and to communicate them to the wider public. This was a "sacred obligation," as the survivor-historian Joseph Kermish put it, supremely important because scholarship would be the antidote to "emotions and prejudices" that infused the subject. The truth about the recent past would shape the future of the Jewish people. The events of the Holocaust, Kermish added, "should … serve as a silent admonition and warning that we must draw national conclusions for future generations." Popular literature, Kermish and his colleagues felt, was simply not up to this task.

Such were the views of scholars and theorists who pondered Yad Vashem's role in formulating the lessons of the Holocaust. Meanwhile, harder men, sometimes more practical leaders, and it must also be said those for whom issues of the Holocaust still cried out for resolution, had their own things to say. For Ben Gurion, the founding father of his country, the main challenge was putting the new state on a secure footing – a task that required attention to long-range goals and strategic alliances, a pragmatic search for allies, cooperation with the new German state in Europe, and an unwillingness to be mired in recriminations over the past, whether at home or abroad. Understandably, this suggested an avoidance of the Holocaust, a cauldron of grief, anger, and unresolved questions. But many felt otherwise. They had scores to settle – with Germany, principally; with the British, charged with closing the gates of Palestine while the Nazis rampaged in Europe and inhibiting the growth of the Jewish state; with states deemed to have collaborated in the Final Solution or to have refused calls for rescue; and also with Jews who were deemed to have escaped proper retribution for what they had done or not done during the Holocaust. In the latter view, such betrayers even included leaders of the Palestinian Jewish community during the dark years, who were charged with "Palestinocentrism," that is, focusing exclusively on the building of the Jewish homeland rather than confronting the British more aggressively or prioritizing the rescue of Jews in Nazi-dominated Europe; or those who had allegedly collaborated with the Nazi enemy, either through participating in the Jewish Councils, or *Judenräte*, or the Nazi-imposed Jewish police, or as *Kapos*, assisting in the management of concentration or death camps; or those who negotiated with the Nazis, ostensibly to save Jews, but in reality, according to those who pursued this line, to enrich and empower themselves and to save their associates, family members, and a privileged elite.

Issues relating to the Jews' wartime ordeal burst into postwar public attention from time to time – among the most spectacular being the bitter, protracted debates in the early 1950s over the Israeli government's eventually successful efforts to conclude a Holocaust reparations agreement with German chancellor Konrad Adenauer. Notwithstanding the difficult negotiations and the reluctance of many Israelis to accept negotiations with the Germans, Ben Gurion managed to carry the day, famously describing his policy with a biblical verse, "Let not the murderers of our people also be their inheritors." Angry opponents, led by Menachem Begin, then leader of the right-wing Herut Party, construed the agreement as tantamount to a pardon of Germany for the murder of European Jews. Other clashes centred on accusations of alleged wartime Jewish misbehaviour, sometimes against individuals accused of having been accomplices of the Germans and committing various offences during the war. The most serious was the affair of Rudolf

Kastner, in the middle of the decade, when that Hungarian Zionist leader, closely associated with the ruling Labour Party, brought a libel suit against an angry polemicist, Malkiel Grunewald, who had accused him, and by implication the Labour establishment, of having collaborated with the Nazis during the war and betraying Jewish victims. Kastner's failure to secure the conviction of his tormenter, his subsequent assassination in 1957, and the High Court's eventual reversal of the decision against him in the libel action were all noisy, bitter public clashes. Israel in the 1950s was a bustling, generally forward-looking place, absorbing many tens of thousands of Holocaust survivors and constructing the institutions of the fledgling state, but it was also fertile soil for bitter recrimination, the weaving of conspiracy theories about what was done and what was not done and what ought to have been done during the war, and tempestuous polemics over what the Holocaust taught, how people should think about it, and what should be done about those who had yet to be judged.

Hanna Yablonka, the Israeli historian of the Eichmann trial, notes contrasting reactions within the country in May, 1960, when Ben Gurion announced to the Knesset that Adolf Eichmann, "who was responsible, together with the Nazi leaders, for what they called 'the final solution of the Jewish problem' in other words – the annihilation of six million of Europe's Jews," had been captured and brought to Israel for trial. In the general public, there was pandemonium – and as often with great historic events, Israelis remember to this day where they were when they heard the news. "Shock, pride, satisfaction, verbal letting off of steam, anticipation, and the feeling that justice should be carried out under the law" – all these strong reactions jostled together. Among Holocaust survivors, however, numbering some half a million and constituting one-quarter of the country's entire population, Yablonka continues, responses were more sombre, subdued, and complicated. Their satisfaction at the news, she summarizes, included "a large measure of sadness, pain, and frustration."

The ambivalence among so many survivors was due to their often disheartening experience of their reception in Israel. For the
truth was that, notwithstanding the Yishuv's and then Israel's
eager acceptance of so many victims of the Holocaust during the
postwar period and the War of Independence, survivors had not
in general had an easy time in the new Jewish state. The new country found it difficult to fit them into the new national narrative.
In her book on these issues, historian Idith Zertal refers to the period as one of "buried memory." For the most part, the stories of
Holocaust survivors remained discreetly out of the national lime-
light. As Israeli journalist Tom Segev summarizes, "The Holocaust
came to be seen as a Jewish defeat. Its victims were censured for
having let the Nazis murder them without fighting for their lives
or at least for the right to 'die with honor.' This attitude in time
became a sort of psychological and political ghost that haunted the
State of Israel – reflecting scorn and shame, hubris and dread, in-
justice and folly." In the Hebrew slang of the day, Holocaust survivors were sometimes called *sabonim*, which some say refers to the
soap that was believed (mistakenly, it turned out) to have been fab-
ricated from Jewish corpses by the Germans, and which others say
derives from a colloquial Hebrew term for weaklings – in either
case, a term of cruel deprecation. In this atmosphere, Holocaust
remembrance was mainly consigned to religious groups. Fanfare
was avoided. The country's attention to survivors, for the most
part, went to Holocaust heroes – leaders of ghetto uprisings and
partisan formations, understood as having engaged in a common
struggle with those who had battled for a Jewish state in Palestine.
Survivors were not part of the national pantheon.

Eichmann's abduction in Argentina and his dispatch to Israel,
his trial and eventual execution brought the country's conception
of the wartime catastrophe to an entirely different level, capturing
the attention of Israelis as no other domestic public event, before or
since. The impact upon the young country was profound. Certainly
the Israeli leadership was conscious of the spectacle's importance –
although when the affair began few could have predicted just how
profound its impact was going to be. What conclusions Israelis
drew from it, however – and what lessons it promoted – were of

course another matter, and historians debate these matters to this very day.

Practically minded, the Israeli prime minister riveted upon the consolidation of the thirteen-year-old Jewish state. Ben Gurion had not been among those who had dwelt upon Holocaust themes. Yehiam Weitz, one of the students of this subject, notes that the prime minister had been very little involved in the Kastner affair or other Holocaust-related issues of the 1950s. It is unclear that Ben Gurion had any idea, when Eichmann was captured, that his trial would constitute an important turning point in the national consciousness of his countrymen. Much has been written about Ben Gurion's declared goals for the Eichmann trial and his eagerness to harness it to national objectives. Hannah Arendt embraced this view, seeing the Israeli prime minister as the moving force behind bringing Eichmann to Jerusalem and what she called "the invisible stage manager of the proceedings" against him. Arendt certainly exaggerated, and in fact the Israeli prime minister was very little preoccupied with the details of the case. But Ben Gurion *did* interfere in the trial. In what was a highly irregular procedure to say the least, the Israeli prosecutor Gideon Hausner submitted his opening speech to the prime minister beforehand. Ben Gurion demanded several changes related to the country's relationship with West Germany, all of which were intended to distinguish between ordinary Germans and the perpetrators of the Holocaust. The Israeli prime minister wanted the word "Nazi" added to the word "Germany" to assert the distance of Nazism from the German people; he wanted Hausner to omit a claim that Nazism was inevitable in Germany; and he wanted to emphasize the role of Hitler in German criminality rather than that of ordinary citizens. All of these points were intended to facilitate Israel's domestically controversial engagement with the new German state – even though Israel and West Germany had no diplomatic relations at this point. And so there was no little irony and no little concern with lessons. "Here was a leader dictating the historiography of his people," Segev observes – quite remarkable for a prime minister who had so assiduously avoided Holocaust issues in the preceding period.

Ben Gurion's central preoccupation was state building. As Israel's veteran Zionist and most powerful political founder saw it, the purpose of the trial was to solidify Israel's standing at home and abroad. The trial, he told the *New York Times*, would "make the details of his case known to the generation of Israelis who have grown up since the holocaust" (*sic*). These facts, which he implied constituted a "lesson" in themselves, were unashamedly nationalist and related to Israel's future generation rather than to settling the scores with Germany or the Second World War. "It is necessary that our youth remember what happened to the Jewish people. We want them to know the most tragic facts in our history, the most tragic facts in world history. I don't care whether they want to know them. They should be taught the lesson that Jews are not sheep to be slaughtered but a people who can hit back – as Jews did in the War of Independence."

Ben Gurion also wanted to secure international recognition of the Jewish state and to have it accepted globally as "the heir of the murdered Six Million, the only heir," as he wrote to Joseph Proskauer of the American Jewish Committee. Beyond this, the obligation to "remember" extended to the world at large. Pointedly, he wanted the world to be *ashamed*. And this had everything to do with Israel and its place in the international community.

> We want to establish before the nations of the world how millions of people, because they happened to be Jews, and one million babies, because they happened to be Jewish babies, were murdered by the Nazis. We ask the nations not to forget it. We want the nations of the world to know that there was an intention to exterminate a people. That intention had its roots in anti-Semitism. They should know that anti-Semitism is dangerous, and they should be ashamed of it. I believe that through this trial all thinking people will come to realize that in our day the gas chamber and the soap factory are what anti-Semitism may lead to. And they will do what they can about it.

Linked with these basic objectives was Ben Gurion's case for Israeli jurisdiction – something sharply questioned internationally because of Eichmann's kidnapping by Israeli agents in Argentina and their flying him to Israel for trial. In the lead-up to the pro-ceedings, Ben Gurion was outspoken in justifying Israel's judicial standing. For the prime minister it was essential that the country's own legal institutions take charge of prosecuting a crime against the murdered millions, and by implication the Jews worldwide. "The Holocaust that the Nazis brought down upon the Jewish peo-ple is ... a unique and unparalleled affair, an intentional attempt to totally exterminate all the Jewish people in the world," he said. "It is the duty of the State of Israel, the only sovereign authority of the Jews, to tell in the greatest detail all there is to know about its scope and dreadfulness, without disregarding the other crimes against humanity of the Nazi regime, not however as one of the items of these crimes, but as a unique crime that has no parallel in the his-tory of mankind." "In my opinion, the punishment is not impor-tant," he told a cabinet meeting. "There is [no] punishment for the murder of 6,000,000 Jews. But what we want to do is to tell the whole story before the Jewish people, because the Jewish case has not been recounted, not even in the Nuremberg Trials."

While preoccupied with international objectives, Ben Gurion's strategy also had its internal Jewish political context. This in-volved his bitter quarrel with the president of the World Zionist Organization, Nahum Goldmann, over the nature of the trial. Suave and sophisticated, Goldmann was an imposing personality who made a powerful case for Diaspora Jewish interests as a coun-terpoise to those of Israel and his great rival, the Israeli prime min-ister. Countering Ben Gurion, Goldmann spoke up very shortly after Eichmann's capture, arguing that, while the accused should be brought before an Israeli judge, the court should be enlarged by other judges, coming from other countries whose citizens had been murdered. Ben Gurion responded furiously, condemning this pro-posal as an affront not only to the Jewish state but also to Jewish honour. The prime minister's response was as blunt as his history, notes Tom Segev. In a nutshell, "the Holocaust happened because the Jews did not live in their own country." At a heated meeting, Ben Gurion famously accused Goldmann of being "neither an Israeli nor an American, but a wandering Jew."

Ben Gurion had little time for historical lessons. Unlike his opponents, he wasted no effort building analogies. "The world has
changed since 1945," he wrote in response to an inquiry. "The ruling forces in the world are not the same. We cannot bring back the
six million, who were slaughtered and burnt in Europe, but in the
Middle East, in Egypt and Syria, the Nazi disciples wish to destroy
Israel – and this is the greatest danger now facing us, and we must
withstand it."

When the trial opened on the morning of April 18, 1961, the
prosecution had its strategy in place: it would be the survivor-
witnesses, not the lawyers, who would communicate what the
Holocaust was all about. In a moving presentation of the prosecution's case, Israeli attorney general Gideon Hausner began with
a lengthy address that spanned the history of the Holocaust and
Eichmann's purported role in it. Clad in a simple black robe, occasionally pointing at the accused in a protective glass booth, he
addressed the court – "Judges of Israel," he called them – in a voice
that had biblical resonance.

> When I stand before you here, Judges of Israel, to lead the Prosecution
> of Adolf Eichmann, I am not standing alone. With me are six million
> accusers. But they cannot rise to their feet and point an accusing finger
> towards him who sits in the dock and cry: "I accuse." For their ashes are
> piled up on the hills of Auschwitz and the fields of Treblinka, and are
> strewn in the forests of Poland. Their graves are scattered throughout
> the length and breadth of Europe. Their blood cries out, but their voice
> is not heard. Therefore I will be their spokesman and in their name I will
> unfold the awesome indictment.

In the jurist Lawrence Douglas's acute analysis of the prosecution's case, this was Hausner's way to "teach history lessons,"
both to the Israelis and to the world. "Hausner treated the Nazis'
central crime as both the act of physical annihilation and the more
profound attempt to erase memory itself – both of the cultural life
of a people and the crimes of the final solution. The act of creat-
ing an opportunity for the public sharing of the narratives of the

survivors, the proxies of the dead, was itself a way of doing justice." In contrast to the trial before the International Military Tribunal at Nuremberg fifteen years before, the case against Eichmann did not rest upon documents, which had been the American strategy, but rather upon scores of survivors who gave detailed and sometimes anguished accounts of what they had endured.

Historians have noted that Ben Gurion's appreciation of the impact of the trial on the Israeli public actually grew during the lengthy preparation of the trial and the proceedings themselves. Once these began, their effect on the Israeli public at large took on a momentum of its own. Close to eighty thousand Israelis attended the trial at one point or another, and some seven hundred journalists from every part of the globe covered the proceedings. Tens of thousands throughout the country heard occasional live transmission of testimony of witnesses and daily wrap-ups by leading journalists of Kol Yisrael, the national broadcaster, in the evenings, following the daily news. In buses, shops, and street corners, normal social interaction stopped whenever people heard these transmissions from the courtroom. Political strategists seem to have been caught unaware: they had no idea that the radio would move so many people so powerfully and actually had no prearranged strategy to orchestrate this. Outside Israel, the Eichmann trial was a major television event; at home, Ben Gurion had not believed in television and had even vetoed its introduction in the Jewish state. Like most others, the Israeli prime minister seems to have been surprised at the degree to which the testimony of so many survivors touched the psyche of the Israeli public, marking an important step in the country's receptivity to a new public discourse on the Holocaust.

More than this: as Annette Wieviorka puts it, at the Eichmann trial the survivor witnesses came to centre stage for the first time. "The trial in Jerusalem was in theory the trial of a perpetrator. But Eichmann quickly disappeared. The attention of the media was no longer directed at the protagonist of the 'final solution.' The man in the glass booth was eclipsed by the victims." Thanks to the survivors' testimony, Holocaust recollections were validated nationally and attended to by a receptive public as never before. Radio seems to have played a crucial role in this process. What the survivors had to tell was disembodied, stripped down to voices, unmediated by age, broken spirits, or expressions of pain. "Taking to the airwaves meant an opportunity to speak away from the tattooed, traumatized body, clear of the label of madness and unintelligibility," write two Israeli researchers, Amit Pinchevsky and Tamar Liebes. "By removing survivors' voices from their bodies radio effectively redefined the conditions by which trauma could find public articulation." The trial also gave a major boost to the writing and publishing of new memoirs – a process that continues even to our own time, when the ranks of survivors have thinned. Public discourse about the Holocaust, including films, literature, and other works of art, followed, together of course with media interest, historical research, and more popular writing on the subject.

In their judgment at the trial's conclusion, the three-judge panel returned briefly to the issue of lessons, even as they limited their determinations to matters having strictly to do with the charges against the accused. "What is the lesson which the Jews and other nations must draw from all this, as well as every person in his relationship to others?" the judges asked. In their response, the jurists famously refused to pronounce. "The Court ... cannot allow itself to be enticed into provinces which are outside its sphere," they said. "The judicial process has ways of its own, laid down by law, and these do not change, whatever the subject of the trial may be ... Accordingly, [the court's] ability to describe general events is inevitably limited. As for questions of principle which are outside the realm of law, no one has made us judges of them, and therefore no greater weight is to be attached to our opinion on them than to that of any person devoting study and thought to these questions." In a rare moment of temptation to define its *own* lessons, the court said no.

Yet as virtually no one had fully expected, the Eichmann trial promoted a sense of shared cultural trauma, something that has become a central element in the national consciousness ever since. And this, inescapably, was its Zionist message. "All of us should bear the enormity of the Holocaust and its mandatory lesson for the nation's retention of its country," said Hausner about the core message of the proceeding. "We must cling to this country, preserve and support every stone and rock, since it is our last refuge."

And with all of this came debate and discussion on all levels, with all kinds of themes, and among them more than a few who framed their views as the lessons of the Holocaust. "Thanks to Eichmann," writes David Cesarani, "'the Holocaust' gelled and became part of the civil religion of Israelis, for good and for ill." And the lesson-teaching did not stop there. The Israeli attorney Michal Shaked, author of a sensitive study of Justice Moshe Landau, the presiding judge of the Eichmann court, had his own lesson to teach, namely that Israel was a country where the rule of law prevailed. Shaked, drawing on Landau's private memoirs, shows how deeply committed this jurist was to his lesson, and how successful he was in pursuing it.

In the years following the Eichmann trial, the Holocaust infused Israeli national identity, its role and intensity shifting according to the prevailing national self-image, as sociologists Daniel Levy and Natan Sznaider put it. Avraham Burg, the former speaker of the Israeli Knesset and an Orthodox Jew, makes a similar case. "The Shoah is more present in our lives than God," he writes. Grounding this astonishing statement, Burg draws upon a poll of teaching trainees in Tel Aviv, in which more than 90 per cent of respondents said that the Holocaust was "the most important experience of Jewish history." Burg is hardly sanguine about what Israelis draw from this preoccupation. "Politicians use it as a central argument for their ethical manipulations. People on the street experience daily the return of the horrors, and newspapers are filled with an endless supply of stories, articles, references and statements that emanate from the Shoah and reflect it back into our lives."

Burg is not the first to make this point. "From the day you were born in Israel," observes Etgar Keret about the larger context for his countrymen, "you've been taught that what happened in Europe over the past few centuries was nothing but a series of persecutions and pogroms, and despite the dictates of common sense, the lessons of that education continue to fester somewhere in your gut." The Holocaust, says Israeli historian Steven Aschheim, echoing the views of many, "has become a defining, almost obsessive fact of our consciousness." And remarkably, far from diminishing over time, this preoccupation becomes, if anything, more intense year by year. In January 2012, *Haaretz* reported on a poll of Israeli Jews on their religious views. "The guiding principle" of Israeli Judaism, they found, is "to remember the Holocaust." Ninety-eight per cent of respondents, reported a popular journalist, Merav Michaeli (the granddaughter of Rudolf Kastner), consider it either fairly important or very important to remember the Holocaust, attributing to it even more weight than to living in Israel, the Sabbath, the Passover seder and the feeling of belonging to the Jewish people. Michaeli concludes: "The Holocaust is the primary way Israel defines itself. And that definition is narrow and ailing in the extreme, because the Holocaust is remembered only in a very specific way, as are its lessons. It has long been used to justify the existence and the necessity of the state, and has been mentioned in the same breath as proof that the state is under a never-ending existential threat." At times, in moments of national peril, public anxiety prompts a quest for guidance from what are described as the lessons of the Holocaust and seeks to situate the dangers faced in that context. Sometimes, conflicting interests battle for legitimacy by asserting the applicability of Holocaust analogies – either with the persecuted, for example, or with struggles for justice in the face of local, national, or global indifference. Campaigners seeking to dramatize their grievances, for example, might appear in striped uniforms as concentration camp inmates or wear yellow stars to associate themselves with the persecuted. Thereby issues, sometimes highly contested, become even more difficult, and responding to them with equanimity, like the Holocaust itself, seemingly impossible.

The most powerful invocations of the Holocaust have involved matters of national security that engage, or are said to engage, the country's physical existence. In June 1967, five years after the Eichmann trial, Israelis faced what seemed to many such a threat in the lead-up to the Six-Day War. Partly at issue, although in the background, was Israel's fear of a "new Holocaust" perpetrated by a dangerously equipped, possibly even nuclear-armed Egypt. Then came immediate threats in rapid succession. In May, Egyptian president Gamal Abdel Nasser concentrated heavy armour and troops along Israel's southern border, dismissed the UN buffer force separating his soldiers from the Israelis, and closed the Straits of Tiran to Israeli shipping and thus to the country's southern port of Eilat. Should Israel launch a war, Nasser warned as he assembled his allies, "it will not be a limited war. Egypt will, thanks to this war, at long last wipe Israel off the face of the earth. We have waited for this moment for eleven long years," he said. Anxiety tightened its grip, Israeli reserves mobilized, and Holocaust-related analyses became a major way of assessing the conflict. This became known as the "waiting period." Jordan joined Syria and Egypt as tensions rose. References to the Holocaust were constant. "During those weeks of drumbeating, the newspapers continually identified Nasser with Hitler," writes Tom Segev. "The proposals to defuse the crisis by any means other than war were compared with the Munich agreement forced on Czechoslovakia before World War II."

After some weeks, on June 5, 1967, Israel launched its long-awaited pre-emptive strike against the Egyptians, routing their air and ground forces, sweeping through the Sinai, and, as the Jordanians, Syrians, and an Iraqi expeditionary force entered the conflict, Israeli soldiers captured East Jerusalem, Gaza, the West Bank, and the Golan Heights as well. Thereby, Israelis found themselves in control of three times as much territory as prewar Israel, along with nearly a million inhabitants living there. Victory, notes Segev, just as with the threat of war, was associated with the Holocaust. Uri Ramon, a young Israeli officer, described his particular experience, which reflected a widespread sentiment:

> Two days before the war, when we felt that we were at a decisive moment and I was in uniform, armed and grimy from a night patrol, I came to the Ghetto Fighters Museum at Kibbutz Lohamei Hagetaot. I wanted to pay my respects to the memory of the fighters, only some of whom had reached this day when the nation was rising up to defend itself. I felt clearly that our war began there, in the crematoriums, in the camps, in the ghettos, and in the forests.

In the wake of this spectacular success, it was easy to avoid critical thought about the place of the Holocaust and its lessons for Israeli society. Victory seemed to provide its own legitimation. Historians have described a brief period of introspection, during which many Israelis contemplated both their shattering insecurities associated with the Holocaust and their euphoric sense of achievement. Self-doubt did not last long, however, and the Six-Day War was followed by the War of Attrition in 1969–70, with intermittent hostilities conducted by Egypt; the murder of Israeli Olympians at Munich in 1972; and another, less successful war for the Israelis, when in 1973, on Yom Kippur, a coalition of Arab countries led by Egypt and Syria attacked territory occupied by the Jewish state. This war was almost certainly Israel's greatest trauma since its inception. During the first days of fighting, Egyptian troops stormed across the Bar Lev Line fortifications along the Israeli side of the Suez Canal that it had captured in 1967, while in the north, Syrian soldiers swept across Israeli defences in the Golan Heights. Thousands of Israeli soldiers were killed, and its air force suffered heavy losses. The country's leadership seemed shaken. Although the Israelis soon recovered and turned the tide of battle, their Holocaust preoccupations not surprisingly persisted, with the sense that the country was constantly under siege.

Among the most chilling and persistent reminders of the linkage of security matters with the Holocaust was a rhetorical reference to "Auschwitz borders," a conflation of the Holocaust past with a geopolitical threat to Israel that came into life only two years after the Yom Kippur War and continues to this very day. The idea was that withdrawal from the conquered territories could precipitate nothing less than Auschwitz-scale massacres, a nightmare come to life. The story of the "Auschwitz borders" began in a speech to the United Nations by Israel's famous diplomat Abba Eban, who addressed the General Assembly in 1975, explaining Israel's apprehensions about returning to the *status quo ante*:

> We have openly said that the map will never again be the same as on June 4, 1967. For us, this is a matter of security and of principles. The June map is for us equivalent to insecurity and danger. I do not exaggerate when I say that it has for us something of a memory of Auschwitz. We shudder when we think of what would have awaited us in the circumstances of June, 1967, if we had been defeated; with Syrians on the mountain and we in the valley, with the Jordanian army in sight of the

sea, with the Egyptians who hold our throat in their hands in Gaza. This
is a situation that will never be repeated in history.

From Eban's explanation of Israeli anxieties, however, there was
considerable distance to travel to argue that withdrawal from the
territories under *any* circumstances might entail a mortal danger
– indeed, might precipitate genocide. However, many promoted
just this vision. Over the years, Israeli settlers have marched and
protested against trading land for peace accompanied by chants
of "Auschwitz borders." Recently, others have denounced American president Barack Obama, who argued for a pulling back to the
1967 armistice lines with mutual territorial swaps, as favouring
"Auschwitz borders." And in the most egregious instance that I
have found, the rightist Zionist Organization of America actually
declared in 2011, "We won't return to Auschwitz!"

Following the Yom Kippur War in 1973, in which Israeli un-
preparedness had exposed the country to the gravest dangers,
Israelis began a national debate which author Yossi Klein Halevi
has called "a decades-long internal war of atonement." How could
the Jewish state have been so overwhelmed in the earliest days of
the fighting? Left and Right developed their own responses. To
the former, the lesson was that political leaders had been arrogant,
unresponsive to Egyptian offers, and over-reliant on force; to the
latter, the problem was Israeli disunity, irresolution, and illusory
hopes for peace. In this clash, reference to the Shoah came natu-
rally to an Israeli Right that had long stigmatized the Left for its
alleged relinquishing of historic claims. In 1974, supporters of a
greater Israel and aggressive colonization of newly occupied territories coalesced around the religiously inspired extremist Gush
Emunim (Bloc of the Faithful) movement, drawing adherents from
the Labour Left as well as the extreme Right. This movement infused its settlement activities with religious and Zionist energies,
contributing to the decline of Labour and the rise of a hard-line
Menachem Begin and the right-wing Likud, closely associated
with the rhetoric of the Holocaust. And to their right was an extremist American rabbi, Meir Kahane, whose Kach ("Thus!") Party
was if anything even more disposed than was the Likud to invoke
the Holocaust as exemplifying Jewish vulnerability. It was Kahane

who coined the term "Never Again," which was taken up by Begin and his political allies. Another consequence of the debate was a growing distrust of the previously dominant Labour Party as insufficiently assertive of Israeli national priorities. In 1977, Begin's electoral success and the advent of a coalition of the Right and the religious parties solidified settlement policies and prompted an increasing recourse to Holocaust-related justifications for aggressive responses to Palestinian terror and violence.

These inclinations accompanied the erosion of Israeli self-confidence after the Yom Kippur War. Such sentiments no doubt contributed in themselves to the intensification of Holocaust-related rhetoric in Israel. But there was also a personal element, namely the powerful impact of Menachem Begin himself. The Shoah personally and deeply marked the Likud leader, whose parents and brother were murdered during the war and who barely escaped with his own life. Quite unlike his great rival, Ben Gurion, for Begin the Holocaust was continuing reality. "Begin thought about the victims, while Ben Gurion thought about the survivors," writes the Likud leader's biographer, Avi Shilon. "Begin sought to restore the national honor and the memory of those who had perished, while Ben Gurion looked to the future; throughout Begin's life the Holocaust was a present reality that served to strengthen his convictions and toughen his spirit, while Ben Gurion emphasized that after the State of Israel had gained its independence the Holocaust became a distant memory, and he wanted Jews to look at the impressive aspects of their people's past." Aluf Benn, editor-in-chief of *Haaretz* at the time of writing, similarly contrasts Begin's preoccupations with those of his Labour predecessors:

> The leaders of Israel in 1973, Golda Meir and Moshe Dayan, did not speak about the Holocaust even during the hardest days of the war. Golda, who believed in the importance of public relations no less than Netanyahu, said at the time to foreign reporters: "Our neighbors are fighting to destroy us." Golda said we know that surrender means death, the destruction of our sovereignty and the physical destruction of all our people. In the Knesset she said: "This is a war over our existence as a nation and a people." But at the time she did not compare Anwar Sadat or Hafez Assad to the Nazis.

Menachem Begin was quite different. In what became his political signature, he made repeated reference to the destruction of European Jewry. From crisis to crisis, Segev observes, "the lessons of the Holocaust were to guide national policy, to serve as a political ideology and emotional alternative to Ben-Gurion's pragmatism." So it was not only with reference to the European countries whose complicity in the Holocaust he repeatedly referenced, but also to Israel's enemies in the Middle East, whom he regularly associated either with a pro-Nazi past or with Nazi-like goals and aspirations. So it was when he justified the Israeli bombing of the Osirak Iraqi nuclear reactor in Baghdad in 1981, and with his open hostility on the diplomatic stage to PLO leader Yasir Arafat, and with his justification of the Israeli invasion of Lebanon in 1982, his cracking down on Palestinian militants, and his ceaseless attack on the weaknesses of the Oslo Peace Accords concluded in 1993.

References to the lessons of the Holocaust continue to reverberate in Israeli society, both for critics of the Jewish state at home and for its defenders abroad. Some years ago, the Nobel Prize–winning Portuguese novelist José Saramago drew extraordinary attention to himself when, on visiting the West Bank city of Ramallah, he compared the place to the Nazi death camp of Auschwitz. Observers were shocked when this happened, in 2002, but more than a decade later I fear that the use of such analogies by opponents of Israel has become almost commonplace, and on the internet and in electronic and print media such extravagant rhetoric is now a fairly regular occurrence. Israeli critics of occupation policies are often similarly preoccupied with the Holocaust. *Haaretz* periodically carries articles criticizing Israelis for ignoring Holocaust lessons in the country's treatment of Palestinians. The Israeli writer A.B. Yehoshua once told an interviewer that Israelis' failure to appreciate the wrongs done to occupied Palestinians made it easier to understand how Germans could claim, during the Holocaust, that they did not know what was happening.

Amira Hass is a controversial, left-wing Israeli journalist who writes about the West Bank and Gaza, and for years she was the only Israeli actually living among Arabs in the occupied territories. The daughter of Holocaust survivors, she has edited a concentration camp diary her mother kept about her time as an inmate of

Bergen Belsen after being captured by the Germans in Yugoslavia. She told all this recently to a reporter who asked about her motivations. "I have a dread of being a bystander," she explained. "Israeli activists opposing their country's treatment of the Palestinians have likened checkpoints in the Occupied Territories to those at the Warsaw Ghetto bridge and other humiliating gestures of control during the course of the Holocaust." As one critic put it of these analogies, "temptations are strong to replace historical analysis with sentiment."

Holocaust preoccupations are common on the Israeli Right, and never more so than in perceptions of a potentially nuclear-armed Iran, whose prime minister from 2005 to 2013 was Mahmoud Ahmadinejad, a conspicuous Holocaust denier. Israeli Prime Minister Benjamin Netanyahu has been particularly prone to invoke supposed lessons of the Holocaust – or for that matter the lessons of history, speaking in Israel on Holocaust Remembrance Day. "The most important lesson from the Shoah is that murderous evil must be stopped as soon as possible, before it can realize its schemes," he said in 2010, unmistakably invoking the Holocaust while threatening a pre-emptive attack on Iranian nuclear targets. Recently, following a speech to AIPAC, the American pro-Israel lobby group, when Netanyahu brandished a letter of 1944 calling for the bombing of Auschwitz, an article in the *Financial Times* referred to "mounting criticism at home over a small but deeply significant aspect of his international campaign: his frequent references to the Holocaust." Among Israelis who complained was Tzipi Livni, former foreign minister and then a leader of the opposition, who called upon "Netanyahu and his government to stop with the hysterical comparisons." Netanyahu's references to the Holocaust have extended to other threats as well. Speaking to the Knesset in January 2012 on the occasion of International Holocaust Remembrance Day, he said that by allowing genocide to occur in Syria the world had shown that it had not learned the lessons of the Holocaust. Some Israelis, unfortunately, had forgotten those lessons too. The "main lesson of the Holocaust when it comes to our fate," he insisted, was "'We can only rely on ourselves'" – a widely held belief that runs the risk, his critics feel, of becoming a self-fulfilling prophecy.

We cannot know precisely how much weight to assign to Netanyahu's personal predilection for Holocaust rhetoric, for, after all, as we have seen, he reflects a widespread disposition on the Israeli Right to speak in this manner, especially among those, such as the prime minister himself, who see themselves as heirs of Vladimir Jabotinsky, the founder of Zionist Revisionism and a champion of the most militant current of Jewish nationalist thought. Netanyahu's fidelity to much of the Zionist Right's linkage of Israel and the Holocaust, outlined in his 1993 book *A Place among the Nations*, is seen in his situation of the Holocaust in the context of events in the Middle East. In this account, the Arabs are seen as having lent their support to the Nazis' campaign to murder the Jews, and they supposedly continued this objective, along with their Nazi linkages, even after the end of the war. As historian Arye Naor, formerly Begin's cabinet secretary, puts it, "Netanyahu did not interpret the Arab-Israeli conflict in the context of the Holocaust. Rather, he interpreted the Holocaust in the context of the Arab-Israeli conflict." In practical terms, Naor observes, "this means that the Holocaust is not over yet." What is important to note is that for Netanyahu, and indeed for many Israelis, there has been no basic change in the relationship between Jews and their enemies in the global community since the Second World War. "What has really changed?" Netanyahu asked recently. "The hatred of Jews changes form, but it remains – if not [based on] racial superiority, then [on] religious superiority. And the world's apathy toward this hatred remains the same." What has happened is that the world has become accustomed again to those declaring that they want to destroy millions of Jews. The only thing that has changed, he continued, "is our ability and determination to act to defend ourselves and prevent another Holocaust."

In all of this there is the prime minister's unmistakable link to his and his family's Revisionist past. A few years ago, the American journalist Jeffrey Goldberg drew attention to this lineage on the occasion of the one hundredth birthday of Netanyahu's father, Ben-Zion Netanyahu, celebrated at the Menachem Begin Heritage Centre in Jerusalem. (Netanyahu's father died two years later, in 2012.) At that event, the Israeli political élite, including President Shimon Peres, and especially the elder statesmen of the Revisionist movement, gathered to celebrate a living part of their political past. A veteran activist on the Zionist Right and also an academic historian, Ben-Zion Netanyahu was born in Poland, emigrated with his family to Palestine in 1920, and was for years secretary to Jabotinsky, sharing with him a faith in Zionist territorial maximalism and the most uncompromising posture towards Zionism's Arab foes. A prominent historian who taught for many years at universities in the United States, he was deeply imprinted by the Holocaust. His huge masterwork, *The Origins of the Inquisition in Fifteenth Century Spain*, presented a revisionist thesis that the Spanish attack upon Jewish *conversos* in the fifteenth century sprang not from religious hostilities but rather from an essentially racist hatred of Jews, which the victims themselves failed to understand. "Netanyahu wrote in the shadow of the destruction of European Jewry in the mid-20th century, and his words and ideas reflected this proximity," writes Benjamin Gampel, an authority on Iberian Jewry. "[Netanyahu] described the claim of the Inquisitors of rampant Judaizing among the *conversos* as 'atrocity propaganda,' their accusations of heresy as 'big lies' and the group's 'racial theories' as the focal point for those dedicated to 'exterminating' the New Christians." For Netanyahu, Jewish history was a series of repetitions, a "history of holocausts," as he told the *New Yorker*'s David Remnick in 1998.

Attendees watched attentively when the old man rose to speak at the Begin Centre. "His speech, unlike his son's, was succinct, devoid of sentiment, and strikingly unambiguous," observed Goldberg. The short speech focused on Iranian threats that "the Zionist movement will be put to an end and there will be no more Zionists in the world. One is supposed to conclude from this that the Jews of the Land of Israel will be annihilated, while the Jews of America, whose leaders refuse to pressure Iran, are being told in a hinted fashion that the annihilation of the Jews will not include them." What is so remarkable was Netanyahu's repetition of the master narrative of Zionist Revisionism, largely unchanged since the time of the Holocaust. Israel will triumph over her enemies, and will do so by physical and moral strength. "I watched Bibi [Benjamin Netanyahu] while his father spoke," one of the attendees told Goldberg. "He was completely absorbed." So he likely was. Ben-Zion's rhetoric, redolent with the Jewish tragedy, and the insistence on uncompromising determination to prevail seem to have carried his audience of the Right. Many Israelis from elsewhere on the political spectrum would probably have agreed.

While interviewing Israeli war planners for his article, Goldberg noticed dozens of offices with photographs of the three Israeli air force F-15 fighters that staged a thunderous fly-past over the former death camp of Auschwitz in 2003 – a display that unmistakably linked Israeli arms to the history of the Holocaust and the close to a million Jewish victims of that camp. Yehuda Bauer, the leading Israeli historian of the subject, recently excoriated this effort to associate Jewish power with Holocaust commemoration. Auschwitz is, he reminded his readers, the largest Jewish cemetery in the world. To Bauer, the sabre-rattling from on high was an unconscionably vulgar exercise of military might. "You do not brandish flags in cemeteries," he wrote – with obvious reference to some iconic photographs from the March of the Living, "and you do not stage exhibition flights over it. Nor do you stage coordinated performances between a flyover and a ceremony on the ground. For that you have theater. In a cemetery, you tiptoe around and weep out loud or deep down inside. Whoever is religious, prays. The flight over Auschwitz was a childish action, ostentatious, utterly superfluous – one that only underscored the shallowness of those who think the memory of the Holocaust ought to be preserved by such means. For Israel's future, this is the wrong kind of symbol."

The Holocaust has similarly appeared in the passionate debate, in Israel today, about asylum seekers – thousands of people from African countries who have been trying, in recent years, to find refuge in the country. Opinion within the government has run strongly against these claimants. At the time of writing, the country's Ministry of Interior has estimated that over fifty thousand have entered Israel illegally, mainly from Eritrea and Somalia, often on foot, and insisting that they are fleeing life-threatening persecution and murderous attacks at home. Exclusionists protest that a fundamental lesson of the Holocaust is that Israel must preserve its Jewish character, and that a huge influx of foreigners poses an "existential threat" to the country, particularly because of the refugees' concentration in particular neighbourhoods in large urban areas. They insist that the asylum seekers are in fact economic refugees, gravitating to Israel as the closest developed society to which they have access. To deal with this situation, Israel began implementing a Prevention of Infiltration Law in 2012, cracking down on masses of illegal immigrants. Demonstrations followed, and opponents of the asylum seekers pushed back, sometimes with ugly accusations. As the issue has heated, refugee advocates have made the case for openness – invoking the Holocaust, at times, against their opponents, who have also done so, but with precisely the opposite objective in mind.

It seems reasonable to ask whether the constant recourse to the Holocaust facilitates constructive decisions that Israelis can live with. Many worry that preoccupations with the Shoah have crippled Israel's capacities to respond imaginatively to questions of national identity and to seize new opportunities in a flawed global community. "We are fast approaching an intersection where we need to decide who we are and where we are going," writes Avraham Burg. "Are we going to the past, toward which we always oriented ourselves, or will we choose the future, for the first time in generations? Will we choose a better world that is based on hope and not trauma, on trust in humanity and not suspicious isolationisms and paranoia? In this case we will have to leave our pain behind us and look forward, to find out where we can repair ourselves and perhaps even the world."

Can recourse to Holocaust lessons be overplayed in Israeli public discourse? Shlomo Avineri, Israel's most distinguished political scientist, suggests as much with reference to the prime minister. "We wake up every morning to some new threat he has found," he says. "We have grown tired of it." Criticism of Netanyahu's use of Holocaust rhetoric during the recent Israeli election campaign agrees. In December 2014, the Israeli prime minister claimed, as one headline put it, that "hypocritical Europeans have 'learned nothing' from the Holocaust." In the popular daily *Yedioth Ahronoth*, Shimon Shiffer irreverently termed Netanyahu's Holocaust references his "doomsday weapon." "If he cannot be strong against Hamas, Netanyahu can at least be strong against Europe," wrote

the diplomatic correspondent Barak Ravid in *Haaretz*. "All that remains to inflame rightist voters' feelings is to curse the French, the
Belgians or the Irish. When those appear not to be working, he
enlists the Holocaust." At the time, Netanyahu's personal popular-
ity was at an all-time low. Of course, whether the majority of his
countrymen agree with Avineri, Shiffer, Ravid, and others on the
subject of Holocaust lessons remains unclear.

To the late Tony Judt, a stout critic of the place of the Holocaust
in Israeli society, the answer was not to abandon preoccupation
with the Holocaust but to accent its universal resonance.

> We have attached the memory of the Holocaust so firmly to the defense
> of a single country – Israel – that we are in danger of provincializing its
> moral significance. Yes, the problem of evil in the last century, to invoke
> Arendt … took the form of a German attempt to exterminate Jews. But
> it is not just about Germans and it is not just about Jews. It is not even
> just about Europe, though it happened there. The problem of evil – of
> totalitarian evil, or genocidal evil – is a universal problem. But if it is
> manipulated to local advantage, what will then happen (what is, I be-
> lieve, already happening) is that those who stand at some distance from
> the memory of the European crime – because they are not Europeans, or
> because they are too young to remember why it matters – will not un-
> derstand how that memory relates to them and they will stop listening
> when we try to explain.

chapter six

Universal Lessons

During the American presidential election campaign of 2008 in which Barack Obama ran against his Republican opponent, John McCain, an exchange occurred that raised, utterly improbably, a lesson of the Holocaust. Attending one of Obama's speeches in Ohio, a spectator named Samuel Joseph Wurzelbacher questioned Obama about small business taxes. Obama's reply included words to the effect that it served the greater good to "spread the wealth around." In the overheated polemics of the day, this response quickly became a *cause célèbre*, evidence of the Democratic Party candidate's "socialism." As the Republican machine seized upon the encounter, pursuing the "gotcha" strategy of political campaigning, it turned out that the questioner, first presented to the media as a plumber and admirable representative of the middle class, was not quite what he appeared: although Wurzelbacher had once worked for a plumbing contractor, it soon emerged that he was a conservative activist, and had been responsible for some personal tax irregularities in the past. He then made some highly aggressive comments on Mexican immigrants ("Put a damn fence on that border going to Mexico and start shooting ... that's how I feel") that cast into doubt his status as a gentle voice of the common man. Dubbed "Joe the Plumber" by the media, Wurzelbacher became a media sensation, shared a platform with John McCain, and became a candidate in his own right, for Congress, in Ohio's ninth congressional district, eventually losing to his Democratic opponent.

In the summer of 2012, as part of his congressional campaign, Joe the Plumber issued a short video entitled "I Love America," in which he referred to the Holocaust. The issue was guns. In 1939, he claimed, Germany "introduced gun control": consequently, the Jews were disarmed, "could not defend themselves," and six million of them, "and seven million others," Wurzelbacher said, were murdered. Wurzelbacher also mentioned the genocide of one and a half million Armenians, just a few years after Turkey supposedly "introduced gun control" in 1911. The Armenians too were "unable to defend themselves." Needless to say, there was no evidence for either contention.* In the uproar that followed, Jewish groups denounced these claims as "beyond the Pale." Some Republicans were embarrassed. Wurzelbacher himself complained that "there were a lot of whiners out there." His spokesman explained that the candidate was "a student of history" and what he had said was "just historical fact." Most important, Joe the Plumber understood that the Second Amendment to the US Constitution "was always the people's last defense against tyrannical government."

The story of Joe the Plumber relates yet another lesson of the Holocaust: the capacity of American political culture to trivialize via the media, and the disposition to use even the most absurd renderings of Holocaust history for private gain. And the story also demonstrates the quite extraordinary way in which this happens through "lessons" – in this case a lesson for which there was no greater authority than Joe the Plumber, a "student of history." The story has a distinctively American populist flavour, and some of its elements are not easily transportable. One hopes. Happily, the story faded from the media almost as quickly as it appeared – and it did not even revive when Wurzelbacher showed up in Israel a few months after the American election, purportedly to serve as a war correspondent for a conservative cable television network, PJMedia, covering fighting in Gaza.

---

* Expanding on this theme, Wurzelbacher went on to predict that Obama's victory would mean "the death of Israel."

As this tale indicates, the growing presence of the Holocaust in our culture since the 1960s has made it inevitable that the topic will be available to promote any number of causes, including the most improbable. Gradually, as we have become more familiar with its significance, we have seen a corresponding erosion of inhibitions from using supposed lessons of the Holocaust to relieve any number of the world's ills. This prompts the obvious reflection that what is claimed as a lesson is often what is brought *to* the Holocaust rather than what is drawn *from* it – a point that Peter Novick made some years ago in *The Holocaust in American Life*. Opposition to "gun control" is of course only one among many causes that are mischievously brought to the subject, with varying degrees of seriousness. Other examples extend from abortion to bullying in schools, gay rights, military and administrative discipline, animal abuses, excesses of capitalism, the rape of the environment, the harshness of bureaucracy, or what have you. In each case, it is claimed, the Holocaust can teach us how to contend with a great wrong. And from this multiplicity of references come questions that I have tried to raise in this book: What does this explosion of thinking by analogy with the Holocaust say about the popular understanding of the destruction of European Jewry? And does it prompt any wider reflection on lessons of the Holocaust?

What follows are some additional examples of lessons, moving from the vulgar contentions of Joe the Plumber to more serious efforts to link the Holocaust to society's concerns. But while I think it will be evident that with these we are in a qualitatively different mode of inquiry from that of Joseph Wurzelbacher, I believe that these examples reinforce my contention that lesson seeking often misshapes what we know about the event itself in order to fit particular causes and objectives. My point is not so much a rejection of these deductions as it is to illustrate their extraordinary variability, their frequent unreliable basis in historical evidence, and their unmistakable invitation to avoid nuance. In my view, pronouncing Holocaust lessons promiscuously enlists our horror of mass murder and other atrocities to press cases that ought to be able to stand on their own. I turn now to three famous thinkers and their proposed lessons – Hannah Arendt, Zygmunt Bauman, and Elie Wiesel.

Notwithstanding her disdain for popular readings of the wartime slaughter of Jews, in her book on the Eichmann trial Hannah Arendt promoted a Holocaust-related lesson that reflects her preoccupations with totalitarianism and her interest in a theme about which historians have done a great deal of research and writing – assigning responsibility for the Holocaust and identifying *German* responsibility in particular. For whatever reason, this line of argument, which concerned Arendt deeply, has been relatively little discussed by commentators. Arendt raised the subject of responsibility in her discussion of the accused, but she did so as well, albeit briefly, in the case of a German soldier who actually assisted Jews in their time of peril. Reporting on witness testimony at the trial, Arendt raised the little-discussed case of Anton Schmidt, a sergeant in the German army who had secretly helped Jewish underground fighters in Vilna, providing them with identification papers and equipment. Schmidt was arrested, convicted by a court martial, and executed in March 1942.

In Beit Ha'am, the large theatre in Jerusalem that served as the Eichmann courtroom, the Jewish partisan leader Abba Kovner, an Israeli resistance figure and a fine poet, relayed the story of Anton Schmidt to a hushed Israeli audience. Deeply moved, for once, Arendt listened with rapt attention to Kovner's testimony about Schmidt's selfless efforts to aid Jews. For her, this was not merely one event among many in the trial, it was a moment of extraordinary significance for an understanding of totalitarianism, which was her key to the murder of European Jews. In a passage of rare emotion, Arendt reflected on what she heard and its being beamed outside the Jerusalem court. "Like a burst of light in the midst of impenetrable, unfathomable darkness, a single thought stood out clearly, irrefutably, beyond question – how utterly different everything would be today in this courtroom, in Israel, in Germany, in all of Europe, and perhaps in all countries of the world, if only more such stories could have been told."

Arendt's point – she called it a "lesson" – was that Schmidt's reaching out to Jews and thereby exposing what the Nazis intended as "holes of oblivion" constituted a chink in totalitarian armour – a gesture that she pressed passionately upon her readers. Totalitarian aspirations could never completely succeed, Schmidt's deeds taught us. Thanks to the German sergeant and others like him, totalitarian dominion could never be complete. Information would always emerge. Some individuals would always fail to comply. That was why no resistance could be deemed "practically useless" – as was said of Schmidt's efforts. For Arendt,

> [It]would be of great practical usefulness for Germany today, not merely for her prestige abroad but for her sadly confused inner condition, if there were more such stories [as Schmidt's] to be told. For the lesson of such stories is simple and within everybody's grasp. Politically speaking, it is that under conditions of terror most people will comply, but *some people will not,* just as the lesson of the countries to which the Final Solution was proposed is that 'it could happen' in most places but *it did not happen everywhere.* Humanly speaking, no more is required, and no more can reasonably asked, for this planet to remain a place fit for human habitation. (Emphasis in original)

Arendt's lesson drew vigorous criticisms. These did not entail any dispute over Schmidt and his actions – recognized by Yad Vashem in 1964 when the organization named the German soldier one of the "Righteous among the Nations." Rather, commentators challenged Arendt's contentions about his significance. Why was Schmidt's *Germanness* so significant and why should his role be so important for his countrymen? asked one investigator. The point here was to claim that Arendt improperly used this atypical case to cast other Germans in a favourable light. Why should Schmidt be "of great practical usefulness"? asked another. Professor Gertrude Ezorsky, a philosophy professor and one of Arendt's fiercest critics, joined this question to a stinging rebuke of her formulation:

> Let it be noted that when Europe's Jews were being murdered and the toll of Stalin's victims had reached millions, Miss Arendt's political

requirements for this planet were still satisfied. Some people (not most) who faced totalitarian terror were living up to Miss Arendt's moral principles and the Final Solution was not happening *everywhere*. But who with any real moral concern would think that *humanly* speaking nothing more was required, or could reasonably be asked, to make this planet "a place fit for human habitation"?

With respect, I must take just a moment to dissent from the dissent: while I take the point that Arendt's somewhat convolutedly expressed thought in this passage (an obscurity for which she was famous) seems to have given rise to this interpretation, I think what is quoted here refers more to Schmidt's frustration of the Nazis' efforts to hide their crimes completely and to keep the Jews in a "hole of oblivion," than it does to one individual's effort to purge evil from the planet.

In Arendt's defence, the distinguished Berlin-based philosopher Susan Neiman identified Arendt's reference to the German sergeant in *Eichmann in Jerusalem* as "the most moving and memorable passage of the book" – and it is perhaps especially noteworthy that it has received so little attention by comparison with her writing on the Jewish Councils or Eichmann's supposed banality. Neiman notes that Arendt's lesson carries a redemptive message – upon which both historians and critics of all sorts have heaped piles of abuse when it comes to lessons of the Holocaust. In this reading, Arendt was trying to say something about the individual's capacity, even under the most extreme conditions, to resist the power of the state. The notion here, writes Neiman, is that "it is the righteous among us who make the earth habitable [and] someone like Eichmann [who] threatens its moral balance." Anton Schmidt, in this view, was affirming what Jean Améry called trust in the world, something that he had lost forever – and that most people do not expect as a lesson of the Holocaust.

But was Arendt's lesson a deduction "simple and within everybody's grasp"? I think not. Deep in her meditations on the nature of evil, Arendt was comforted by the way in which the story of Schmidt spoke to her as the author of an important book on totalitarianism. Her lesson: people *could* resist. The dominion of totalitarianism was never complete. Is this what people have in mind when they think of lessons of the Holocaust? I doubt it. People seek lessons as calls to action, providing practical guidance to making the world a better place. Instead, claimed her critics, by raising the issue of "practical usefulness for Germany today" Arendt seemed to be suggesting that more Schmidts might have assisted German public relations. Whatever her intentions, this was what her words seemed to convey. And that is why many opposed her "lesson" so vigorously.

Born in 1925, Zygmunt Bauman is a grizzled veteran of the troubled relations among Poles and Jews. A famous Polish-Jewish sociologist who, like many Polish Jews, was part of the Communist apparatus in postwar Poland, he was a fervent supporter of the Soviet-backed regime that set itself up after the war. As these pitiful remnants of Polish Jewry saw it, their main priority was to beat back the nationalist, conservative, and antisemitic forces that contended for power at that time. In the longer run, however, Communism proved very bad for the Jews. In 1968, turned upon by the party with which he had so enthusiastically thrown his lot, Bauman emigrated to Israel and, after a few years, moved to the United Kingdom, where he taught sociology at the University of Leeds. In 1980 he published an influential book entitled *Modernity and the Holocaust*, in which he contended that the destruction of the European Jews was a window onto modern society, a horrible demonstration of how an Enlightenment ideal – the reordering of the natural and man-made environments – could entail monstrous, murderous acts in pursuit of "the design of the perfect society."

For Bauman, Nazism was not a harking back to the barbaric past; rather, it represented, together with the Communist regime of the Soviet Union, a state hell-bent on realizing modern goals and operating without traditional or moral constraints. Each of these regimes sought to construct an ideal, perfect society. Hitler's and Stalin's projects, while differing in the notions of perfection, blended with race on the one hand and class on the other, shared a murderous aspiration:

Stalin's and Hitler's victims were not killed in order to capture and colo-
nize the territory they occupied. Often they were killed in a dull, me-
chanical fashion with no human emotions – hatred included – to enliven
it. They were killed because they did not fit, for one reason or another,
the scheme of a perfect society. Their killing was not the work of destruction, but creation. They were eliminated, so that an objectively better
human world – more efficient, more moral, more beautiful – could be
established. A Communist world. Or a racially pure, Aryan world.

The Holocaust, in this view, was part of a great wave of modernity. Quoting the American rabbi Richard Rubinstein, Bauman saw
"the ultimate lesson of the Holocaust as bearing witness 'to the
advance of civilization.'" "It was an advance," he added, in a dou-
ble sense. "In the Final Solution, the industrial potential and technological know-how boasted by our civilization has scaled new
heights in coping successfully with a task of unprecedented mag-
nitude. And in the same Final Solution our society has disclosed to
us heretofore-unsuspected capacity. Taught to respect and admire
technical efficiency and good design, we cannot but admit that, in
the praise of material progress which our civilization has brought,
we have sorely underestimated its true potential." Bauman had
no time for the idea that the Nazis were monstrous individuals, or
that they deviated from enlightened, liberal notions of progress.
This way of thinking was "self-exculpatory," turning a blind eye
to how modernity was misshaping our own society. Rather, he believed that modernist visions infused modern societies and were
themselves responsible for grotesque attacks on humane values.
Modern activists contemplated society as "an object of administration, as a collection of so many 'problems' to be solved, as a
legitimate target for 'social engineering', and in general a garden
to be designed and kept in the planned shape by force (the garden-
ing posture divides vegetation into 'cultured plants' to be taken
care of, and weeds to be exterminated)." This was, says Bauman,
"the very atmosphere in which the idea of the Holocaust could be
conceived, slowly yet consistently developed, and brought to its
conclusion." He was greatly apprehensive of "the grand design at

the helm of modern state bureaucracy, emancipated from the constraints of non-political (economic, social, cultural) powers."

Following Max Weber, Bauman understood bureaucracy as stripping away the moral obstacles to the pursuit of its objectives – in the case of Nazi Germany, a socially engineered society "meant to bring about a social order conforming to the design of a perfect society." Before this intoxicating vision, previously operating moral standards atrophied. Violence was moved to the fringes of society – "off-limits for a large majority of societies' members; or exported to distant places which on the whole are irrelevant for the life-business of civilized humans." What the Holocaust revealed most of all was the erosion of "pre-existing ethical norms or modern inhibitions." Bauman closed his book with a discussion of "the challenge of the Holocaust," that set off "a feverish search for alternative groundings of ethical principles." What he called for was a reconstruction of a pre-social or supra-social societal morality – notions that he derives from the philosophical anthropology of Emmanuel Levinas.

Part of a significant body of literature that discusses the relationship of modernity to the Holocaust, Bauman's work has generated a cluster of lessons, many of which can be found in his own texts. As with other cases examined here, Bauman's lessons sometimes stand on shaky historical ground and are certainly far from carrying the field of Holocaust historians. To start with the most obvious, most modern states did not emulate the destructive spasms of Nazi Germany or the Soviet Union. Indeed, some of them expended considerable blood and treasure to constrain modernist experiments and destroy their visions. And moreover, many of the worst atrocities of so-called modernist regimes relied in their killing upon primitive technology and method. At the same time, there is a powerful case to be made that modern bureaucracies can and do serve the public good. Enlightenment thinking is not only the preserve of the weeded garden and the egregious atrocity; it is also an arena of tolerance, humanitarianism, and critical analysis. Bauman's views have been battered about by critics who have pursued these and other charges against him, and his work, while respected, has emerged considerably the worse for wear. Clearly, few would want to disarm anyone who sought to mitigate the destructive effects of modernity. But as a universal lesson of the Holocaust this is hardly a call to arms that would win the support of many historians.

Even the most fervent admirers of Elie Wiesel, Nobel Peace Prize laureate and acclaimed as the most prominent spokesman for Holocaust survivors worldwide, would probably appreciate that he is one of the last places to go for lessons of the Holocaust. Of Rumanian background, born in the town of Sighet, he has written over fifty books, and is most famous for his reflections on his experiences in Auschwitz – in recognition of which he was awarded a Nobel Peace Prize in 1986. Speaking of that work, the Norwegian Nobel committee referred to him as a "messenger to mankind." In both his writing and his public addresses, Wiesel's technique is to present an experience, not a road map. His Holocaust communication involves feelings, vignettes, and, very importantly, questions – none of which, in my view, lend themselves to the formulation of lessons. Often, he speaks in parables, making statements that many might challenge and in which his meaning can be susceptible to different interpretations or downright obscure. "While not all the victims were Jews," he famously wrote to US president Jimmy Carter about the new Holocaust Museum, "all Jews were victims." Michael Berenbaum, who worked closely with Wiesel on the Museum, has described the tightrope that Wiesel walked, as chairman of the Holocaust Memorial Council, between Jewish and non-Jewish victims of Nazism. Writing to Carter, he was trying to communicate the particular importance for Jews of the Nazi atrocities against them. But "all Jews were victims"? Note that his claim was not about German *intentions*, but simply that all Jews were victims. How can this be? Surely, those Jews who spent the war safe and sound in North America cannot be counted as victims. Yet the statement lives on, making an explicit claim of universal Jewish victimhood that many refer to as a lesson of the Holocaust – however unreasonably.

For many years Wiesel spoke about the ineffability of the Holocaust – the inability of people who were not "there" to succeed in grasping the murder of European Jews. "Only those who were there will ever know," he has said, "and those who were there can never tell." Pursuing this theme, he spun this message into a kind of winding conversation rather than a description or analysis. In this rhetorical construction, questions are central, and direct the content of his speech. "What was Auschwitz: an end or a beginning, an apocalyptic consequence of centuries-old bigotry and hatred, or was it the final convulsion of demonic forces in human nature?" Who can say? Certainly Wiesel does not, and in the end his discourse can be read as demonstrating the elusiveness of lessons. Does the Holocaust teach pessimism? Well yes, but we must not give in to it. And so we try to be optimistic. Will the world ever learn? It seems not. But then again we must try to teach it. Is the message man's inhumanity to man? No, it was man's inhumanity to Jews. Still, the Holocaust calls us to challenge the evil side of humanity wherever it appears. Might the Holocaust have prompted Wiesel to move to Israel? Yes, but he is unworthy.

Wiesel has been called "the single most influential Jew in America," perhaps the most influential worldwide. In a speech to the United Nations in 2005, on the occasion of its sixtieth anniversary, he came as close as he has to a clear formulation of lessons: "Those who survived Auschwitz advocate hope, not despair; generosity, not rancor or bitterness; gratitude, not violence. We must be engaged, we must reject indifference as an option. Indifference always helps the aggressor, never his victims. And what is memory if not a noble and necessary response to and against indifference?" Are these his lessons from the Holocaust? I have seen them described as such. Many turn to his work precisely in a quest for lessons. But the higher one rises in generality, the less clear are these admonitions as a source of guidance and the less helpful they become in specific instances. And the less reliable they seem as deductions from the circumstances to which they refer. Indeed, few students of the Holocaust would see much connection between Wiesel's frequently articulated questions, his responses, often read as lessons, and the specific events they study. Did generosity accomplish more during the Holocaust than rancour or bitterness? Maybe not. Was gratitude helpful? I can think of plenty of occasions when it wasn't. Was the violence of the Warsaw Ghetto uprising to be condemned? Most would say no, although many Jews elsewhere, still not knowing what lay in store, opposed insurgents for putting entire communities at risk. And, when rejecting indifference, how does one decide where to put one's efforts, which of so many wrongs to oppose? And what about problematic consequences of action? Surely these cannot be ignored. More than once I have served on committees in which the question has been put whether Elie Wiesel might be persuaded to join a particular cause. I do not know if the Holocaust has a lesson that helps him to decide.

Human rights authority and former Canadian Liberal Party leader Michael Ignatieff sums up the remarkable way in which, in our era, outstanding catastrophes like the Holocaust have taken on a universal resonance. "We are scarcely aware of the extent to which our moral imagination has been transformed since 1945 by the growth of a language and practice of moral universalism," he writes. At the beginning of this process, during the 1980s, writers on the Holocaust began to move past one of the important debates that preoccupied some of the pioneers of Holocaust thought such as Elie Wiesel and Emil Fackenheim. Working with a largely blank public slate in the 1960s and 1970s, these writers emphasized the uniqueness of the Holocaust, Fackenheim folding it into his Jewish theology and Wiesel formulating a view of Jewish victimhood through his experience with the camps and evidence of the special obsessiveness of Nazi persecution.

More recently, however, writers seem to prefer universal themes. During the second half of the 1980s in Germany, in the so-called *Historikerstreit*, or historians' debate on the Holocaust, intellectuals went after each other, to considerable media attention, over the question of how the Holocaust should be interpreted and remembered in Germany. Part of this quarrel centred on the notion of the uniqueness of the Nazis' campaign to murder the Jews. Critics of this idea, mainly on the Right, made increasing reference to the validity of comparisons – with the Soviet Union, in the first instance, but eventually also with other cases of genocide, particularly in colonial situations. The implications for lessons were inescapable, although not all realized it at the time. If the Holocaust were unique, it was difficult to see how universal lessons could emerge from it; on the other hand, if the Holocaust could be compared with other instances of mass killing, it might be possible to establish patterns that applied to other situations. At the same time, not all comparisons were valid. But more and more, students of the Holocaust juxtaposed the wartime murder of Jews with the Nazis' other imperial visions and with other episodes of mass killing. While the debate faded in the post–Cold War context, the study of the Holocaust remained vigorous in Germany and benefited substantially from the availability of new archival material made available in former Soviet-dominated countries.

Following the collapse of the Soviet Union and the gravitation of international politics to human rights issues, policies of the Clinton administration in the United States brought Holocaust-related matters to a new level of public attention. A major issue was restitution – the settlement of material claims of survivors of the Holocaust and other Nazi atrocities that had never been properly adjudicated at the end of the Second World War. These claims involved class action lawsuits brought against Swiss banks for so-called "dormant accounts," litigation against German corporations for slave and forced labour, and proceedings against international insurance companies for unpaid policies originally held by murdered victims – all of which were accompanied by detailed, complicated negotiations for settlement. Another issue was Holocaust education and the shaping of its historical memory, themes that assumed quite extraordinary international attention, to a degree that could scarcely have been imagined in the period following the collapse of Nazism and the end of the Second World War. The global linkage, as many observed, was human rights.

Links between the Holocaust and human rights surfaced at an international conference on Holocaust Education Remembrance and Research called by the Swedish Prime Minister Göran Persson and his government, with the support of the Americans, that assembled in Stockholm in January 2000. This meeting, the first in a series organized by the Stockholm International Forum on the Holocaust, brought together twenty-three heads of state or prime ministers and fourteen deputy prime ministers or ministers from forty-six governments, including the Vatican. US Ambassador Stuart Eizenstat, the American representative to the European Union, spoke for his government on Holocaust and human rights issues. As he told the US Senate, it was time to go from questions of money, that is, restitution, to memory: "The last word on the Holocaust should be the memory of its victims and the teaching of its enduring lessons." And because the focus was international – that is, relations between states – American leadership was essential.

In this environment, publicly articulated lessons of the Holocaust shifted from constant analogies with Nazi Germany to global issues of genocide and mass murder that extended beyond the reference point of the Second World War. References to the Holocaust took on a particular American flavour. Eizenstat claimed a special leadership role for the United States to resolve Holocaust issues globally, a process that some have even referred to as "the Americanization of the Holocaust." Understandably, Europeans did not always accept this with equanimity. Some chafed at American claims to be liberators in 1945 when it was the Red Army, and not soldiers of the United States, which liberated the vast majority of Holocaust victims. American claims of moral leadership as the country untainted by responsibilities for the destruction of European Jewry did not necessarily sit well with many Europeans during Holocaust-era restitution campaigns of the 1990s. The problem then was the role assumed by American courts in class action lawsuits, and later in settlement proceedings, to direct a process that mainly affected European governments, corporations, and banks.

These efforts persist – an outstanding example, only recently resolved through a bilateral settlement between the American government and France, involved skirmishes in the United States over claims of some Holocaust survivors against the French National Railways, or SNCF. Particularly vexatious to the French was that plaintiffs only turned to American courts after the failure of such lawsuits in France. Jan Surmann, an astute academic critic of the

Stockholm process, has noted the way in which this global trend "decontextualized Holocaust remembrance," removing it from the countries in which the events transpired and transferring the action to the United States in highly symbolic litigation. "The U.S. politics of history," he writes, "can be understood as instigating a process that transformed the postwar Holocaust narrative and embedded it in a new, transnational meta-narrative wherein the lessons of Auschwitz lead to universal responsibility for human rights." Thereby, the "real historical event [has grown] blurry," and has been "trivialized and dehistoricized."

In the years that have followed the first Stockholm conference on the Holocaust, there has been a significant acceleration of linkages of the Holocaust and human rights, and a vast outpouring of lessons from innumerable institutions and individuals who constitute an echo chamber for an increasingly global discourse on the Holocaust. At the United Nations, secretary general Ban Ki-moon speaks of the lessons of the Holocaust. President Barack Obama does so as well, as does Canadian prime minister Stephen Harper. So do countless dignitaries on countless commemorative occasions in many countries. In London, the Imperial War Museum created a permanent exhibit on the Holocaust, opened by Queen Elizabeth II. National monuments to the Holocaust have appeared in various countries, and a Canadian one, designed by the German architect Daniel Libeskind, is being built in Ottawa. At the domestic level, scores of Holocaust-related institutions in North America have written lessons of the Holocaust into their mission statements. There was constant repetition of Santayana's observation about those who do not remember history, or the comment – often attributed to Edmund Burke, although without conclusive evidence – about evil triumphing when good people do nothing. And with this have come ever more lessons.

None of this considerable Holocaust-related activity has brought us closer to any consensus about the content of lessons. Matters have not been helped by the fact that policy makers and commentators attuned to this new public rhetoric frequently had little knowledge of the Holocaust itself or its German or Jewish or European context. More often than not, the substance of Holocaust lessons is simply assumed, as are the ways in which these lessons will somehow do their work. Universal lessons are a mixed bag, extending from some obvious admonitions about good behaviour to some that are highly controversial, both politically and ethically. Reduced sometimes to slogans, the lessons can become familiar through their packaging, but more often than not, I suspect, are discarded as easily as are advertisements.

Some of the discourse on lessons involves eloquent or rhetorically appropriate commentary. I have always appreciated the radical journalist I.F. Stone's humane observation: "the lesson of the Holocaust is that to treat other human beings as less than human can lead to the furnaces," but I do not hear it so much recently. I am less enthusiastic about the Canadian parliamentarian and human rights lawyer Irwin Cotler's frequently declared "the Holocaust is uniquely evil in its genocidal singularity," the meaning of which escapes me. However, taken as a whole, the category of lessons is remarkably unclear. Part of the problem is that the lessons sometimes contradict each other. Some are predictive. A series of lessons include variations on the theme of Jews being "canaries in the coal mine." Closely related is the claim that the lessons are universal and should be projected globally. From this come lessons to the effect that "it" happened to the Jews, but could happen to anyone. Then, different lessons have been crafted that derive from different victims' Holocaust experiences. Some survivors, as we know, emerged crushed by brutality and indescribable cruelty; others accented small acts of kindness or selflessness that saved their lives. Contrasting lessons emerge from each group. Some readers of Holocaust history might derive from Daniel Jonah Goldhagen a lesson about incorrigible German "eliminationist" antisemitism. But admirers of author Daniel Mendelsohn's finely crafted inquiry into the fate of his murdered relatives in wartime Poland might prefer what the author once told an interviewer for National Public Radio, namely that "anybody is capable of anything" – certainly the most capacious lesson of any that I have encountered in my own reading.

To complicate matters, Holocaust lessons change as new problems arise and new generations consider its history. "The horizon is shifting," I read in a blog produced by the Holocaust and Human Rights Center of Maine, with offices in Portland and Augusta. "With it the role and reach of Holocaust organizations must inevitably evolve." Maine's Holocaust Center offers "a suite of free films, panels and workshops to discuss bullying and a related program of restorative justice," pursuing its mission "to advance the cause of ethical literacy." This sounds like admirable work. But some might well be concerned with the way in which those who oversee such programs are increasingly detached from the Holocaust itself, the event from which they claim to take their inspiration. A related problem is the collapse of distinctions, with differences among all wrongs being presented as simply a matter of degree. All the easier is it, therefore, to misinterpret, distort, or even abandon the history of the Holocaust, the elements of which may seem too remote and too horrifying to pursue without an excessive investment of time and energy. And it is here where we need to underscore the variability of lessons.

This is perhaps best demonstrated through examples. Here are some of the most commonly articulated universal lessons that raise questions for which there are no conclusive answers. I stress that these are examples, hardly an exhaustive list.

The Holocaust as a school for tolerance. Probably the most commonly articulated lesson of the Holocaust, in North America at least, is the idea that studying the Holocaust promotes tolerance, deepening an appreciation of cultural, ethnic, and racial diversity and thus making the world a better place in which to live. This is the explicit commitment of the Simon Wiesenthal Center's Museum of Tolerance in Los Angeles, in which a main exhibition on the Holocaust is accompanied by a "Tolerancenter," where "visitors focus on the major issues of intolerance that are part of daily life." I certainly have no quarrel with admirable objectives such as these. Nor do I have the competence to criticize any primary school curricula in which such education might take place. However, I am more than a little uneasy about museological or educational messages that promote present-day notions of tolerance and diversity, concepts that have virtually no relation to the destruction of European Jewry, by linking them to the Holocaust.

To historians, the idea that "intolerance" or "prejudice" is what the Holocaust is all about would be laughable if this were not a serious matter, maintained seriously by men and women of obvious good will. Let us be clear: people in history have forever been "intolerant" and "prejudiced" by our twenty-first-century, North American definitions, without necessarily slaughtering each other and committing genocide in a manner that practically defies belief for any society. The Holocaust is about mass killing, on a continental scale, of a particular group of victims, and not about intolerance or prejudice. Throughout history, societies have commonly stigmatized, exploited, brutalized, punished, and persecuted groups and individuals – and even worse – without slaughtering them so obsessively or seeking to wipe them off the face of the earth. An important question about the Holocaust is why and how barriers of law and custom and religion seem to have collapsed under the Third Reich and how the Germans managed to organize killing on such a vast scale. Narrowing the Holocaust to an issue of intolerance and prejudice not only prompts a misunderstanding of such wrongdoing in our world today, it also misstates the significance of the event, the authority of which we are then borrowing so disrespectfully.

It began with words. Public personalities who have called for restrictions on hate speech in the media and on the Internet have ahistorically invoked the Holocaust with the claim that "it began with words," suggesting that unfettered speech was a fundamental cause of the Holocaust, if not *the* fundamental cause, and that restrictions on such speech would be an appropriate preventative response, a lesson derived from the Holocaust. Unsurprisingly, this particular lesson seems to have much less currency in the United States, with its extremely robust traditions of free speech deriving from the US Constitution, than in European countries and for that matter Canada, with very different traditions. I have heard this statement hundreds of times, however, on both sides of the Canadian-American border. This contention is subject to the same observations that have been made previously: there are no grounds, historically, for singling out this particular element as a cause of the Holocaust. Rather, doing so distorts the history we claim to be trying to understand. Demonizing others has unfortunately been a common attribute of many societies historically and for that matter exists in many parts of the world today, without the kind of genocidal massacres we associate with the Holocaust. Historians have repeatedly shown how inapt this commentary is for an understanding of the Holocaust. While no one would consider the subject of antisemitism *un*important for a study of Nazism, most historians would certainly challenge the idea that it paved the way for Hitler's rise to power or that it mobilized Germans to a genocidal attack on Jews. Some years ago, historian William Sheridan Allen summed up a historical consensus succinctly when he said that more Germans became antisemites because they became Nazis than became Nazis because they were antisemites. Then, too, claims about the salience of antisemitism dissolve when examined comparatively. Was German antisemitism, for example, any more widespread and venomous than, say, Polish or Hungarian or Rumanian antisemitism? Probably not. And how would it compare, for that matter, with the Canadian antisemitism of the prewar era? George Mosse used to illustrate how useless were Holocaust explanations based on antisemitic reputation. If you were situated in the 1890s and were told that one of the European states of the day would be responsible for a Holocaust, which would you choose? he would ask. More often than not, anyone who knew anything about European antisemitism of that era would probably select Tsarist Russia. And after that, almost certainly France. Germany would not be high on the list. So, why Germany?

All it takes for the triumph of evil is that good men do nothing. Among the most popular of Holocaust lessons, this statement blends good intentions with popular clichés. Just as there are few who would champion hate speech, there are few who believe that good men should "do nothing." But "all it takes"? Doris Bergen puts her own critique well: "The slogan 'all it takes' is a call for civil courage. It urges us to stand up, to speak out against social justice. At the same time, it assumes a softened version of the Holocaust that is politically safe and even comforting, because it involves no killers, only victims and witnesses." Holocaust historians have carefully examined the motivations of perpetrators, the mindset of facilitators, and the politics of collaboration. And they have taken great care to examine the institutional and situational factors that facilitated mass killing. In any assessment of the rise of Nazism or the Holocaust, it would be an outrageous misstatement to claim that "good men did nothing" to oppose Nazism – or even, for that matter, to resist the Germans' carrying out the Final Solution. Too few, certainly. Too late, as is so often the case in human affairs. Without sufficient energy, maybe presumptuous of us to say so. But "all it takes," "did nothing" are bits of slogans, hardly constituting a serious assessment. Worse still, promoting them as a lesson that if "good men" would only act responsibly all may be well not only presents a childishly simple view of how genocide functions but also slights resistance that did occur to no effect whatever.

One person can make a difference. Another distortion of Holocaust history in the service of good intentions is the idea that every individual has the capacity to thwart the evils of a state like Nazi Germany – a notion that would be quite properly scorned by any who actually had to face its unrelenting power. Arguably, the history of daily lives of Jews under Nazism suggests precisely the opposite – how even the most resourceful, the bravest, those who were willing to hurl themselves against the machinery of destruction, more often than not failed even to slow the killing process. Coming from a religious discourse that may celebrate acts of goodness wherever they appear, this claim probably has more to do with our hunger for redemptive messages than anything else. And there are some cruel implications. One of them is that ordinary people ought to have had a clearer vision of what they were facing, or more courage in dealing with it. Or that bystanders ought to have acted more forcefully. But the slightest effort at comparison suggests how fanciful is this idea. Peter Hayes points rightly to the case of Soviet prisoners of war who perished at such staggering rates and numbers – and these were young men, with military training and fighting experience, of whom close to three and a half million, almost 60 per cent of those captured, succumbed to starvation, abuse, and outright massacre. "The contest was so uneven that it is cruel to the memory of the victims to talk of how much they could have gummed up the German operations if only they'd been less cooperative," he says. It may gratify us to identify heroes who sacrificed themselves or who became martyrs to a good cause. We may well choose to identify them as examples. But formulating such cases as lessons of the Holocaust obscures the historical reality of wartime genocide and falsifies the situation that bystanders actually faced.

Siding with victims. "Indifference and inaction always mean coming down on the side of the victimizer, never the victim" goes another familiar slogan. There is a considerable historical discourse on what might have been done to rescue Jews during the Holocaust, and there are specialists in Holocaust lessons who relentlessly pursue long-gone historical actors, charging that they could and should have done more to save the victimized. Who could deny such assertions, in general terms at least? In hindsight, there are few instances, and few individuals, for whom this is *not* true for virtually *every* human-made catastrophe – either in our personal lives or in public affairs. Afterwards, we can almost always identify how things might have been done better. But while in hindsight more could have always been done, and while it can be instructive to engage in such counterfactual history, it is wise to exercise care in doing so. During the Second World War, when so few, including the victims themselves, grasped the reality of the Final Solution, and in the throes of a worldwide conflict of unimaginable destructiveness, people did not have the luxury to act as we might like to think we would act – and as it is so easy imagine them doing now. What is important if we want fully to understand is to assess the situation people faced with as clear-eyed judgment and as full an awareness of the evidence as we can. Disagreement over such things is inevitable. Historians are by no means unanimous that, practically speaking, large numbers of Jews could have been saved from the Nazis' implementation of mass murder, and they also disagree on whether prioritizing rescue was a conceivable choice for decision makers involved in a desperate struggle against the Third Reich.

The strongest part of this argument has to do with the Depression years, when Allied immigration policies turned increasingly towards restrictions in the late 1930s, following the *Anschluss* with

Austria and the events of *Kristallnacht*. Still, in country after country where policies towards Jews have been examined, historians have identified fierce opposition to opening the door to refugees in general and Jews in particular. Once the lethal machinery of destruction began to operate, accelerating powerfully in mid-1941 with the Germans' invasion of the Soviet Union, Jews were almost completely inaccessible to Allied rescue possibilities, and in any event such "humanitarian intervention," as we came to call it in the 1990s, efforts on behalf of millions of people in wartime, was about as foreign an idea to the Allied governments as modern-day human rights might be to the nineteenth-century imperial powers. Such notions were generations in the future. Without prejudging particular cases, those who invoke the Holocaust have an obligation, it seems to me, to assess all of the evidence we can bring to bear, rather than just the evidence that conforms to particular moral injunctions cast as lessons.

Summing up the lessons of the Holocaust I have discussed in this book, I want to clarify some limits of my critique. My quarrel is not necessarily with the probity of any of the purported lessons as various people have drawn them. Some of these may be quite true; many are valuable as admonitions; and people who advance them are often very well intentioned, even exemplary. The problem is not with intentions or goals; the problem is an insufficient acquaintance with Holocaust history. Bullying in the schoolyard is clearly wrong, and it is admirable that some people have taken up this cause. However, my problem with lessons remains, both when people allude to them historically and when they reduce their conclusions to formulae that cannot bear the weight put on them. My problem with such formulae is that they generally do not depend upon the Holocaust for their veracity; nor are they necessarily true in every respect; nor should they necessarily need or depend upon the Holocaust as a source of validation; nor are they always a guide to modern-day challenges; nor do they necessarily follow from an understanding of the Holocaust that is undertaken by

Holocaust historians. And finally, nor do they derive from what I think should be the first responsibility of Holocaust educators and researchers – to get the history right, which is to say to be faithful to the event from which the lesson is claimed to derive. And that, I suggest, is the first test for anyone who claims to speak with authority about this subject – to be as true as we can possibly be to the facts and circumstances of the Holocaust, and to seek as deep and sophisticated and independent-minded an understanding of these events as we can manage.

As I write these lines, my computer's inbox notifies me of today's email harvest from the *Huffington Post* with a bizarre example to add to my list of lessons. It comes from high places. "Antonin Scalia: Holocaust Was Partially Brought About by Judicial Activism," says a headline broadcast on the Web. The story comes from a report in Colorado's *Aspen Times* covering United States Supreme Court Justice Scalia's address to the Utah Bar Association's 2013 summer convention in Snowmass, Colorado. In it, Scalia excoriated judicial activism, as he has so often done in public addresses. In this case, however, the distinguished conservative jurist raised the matter of Nazi Germany. As the *Aspen Times* recorded it,

> Scalia opened his talk with a reference to the Holocaust, which happened to occur in a society that was, at the time, "the most advanced country in the world." One of the many mistakes that Germany made in the 1930s was that judges began to interpret the law in ways that reflected "the spirit of the age." When judges accept this sort of moral authority, as Scalia claims they're doing now in the U.S., they get themselves into trouble.

So far as I can tell from this brief report, Scalia did not *precisely* attribute the Holocaust to judicial activism. Mercifully, his speech was about legal matters, not lessons of the Holocaust. But given the tone and the warm reception of his talk as a call to action (he received a standing ovation), dozens of headline writers were ready to claim that he did.

Scalia's lesson, if that's what it was, will certainly have been forgotten by the time people read these lines. Nevertheless, we may understand his extraordinary claim in the context of a growing comfort with Holocaust analogies and the temptation to make a strongly felt point by packaging it as a lesson of the Holocaust. There is a limit, however, and this is as good a time as any to declare mine. I believe that when speaking about the Holocaust we all have a fundamental duty to be as faithful as we can be to the epoch-making events from which we issue statements that are supposedly validated by the campaign against European Jewry. To me, there is something fundamentally wrong with using the Holocaust so casually as a source of validation, a means by which we seek special authority for courses of action for which we seek support and approval. As acknowledgment of the significance of the Holocaust has increased globally, an unfortunate accompaniment has been a loss of respect for detailed knowledge of what actually happened. I have seen too much of this. My principal lesson of the Holocaust is, therefore, beware of lessons.

chapter 7

Lessons of the Holocaust

Holocaust history admirably meets the standard set by the best modern-day histories of other subjects. Coming from an international community of academics, writers, and students of particular themes, works in this field display, at their best, balance and objectivity, the avoidance of unsubstantiated generalizations, and up-to-date, reliable research. Their authors ask imaginative questions, and provide answers that are firmly grounded in evidence. Typically, the best histories on this subject also avoid overreach – among other things, writing prescriptions for future behaviour meant to apply without qualification in all kinds of circumstances and situations. These prescriptions are what I have referred to in this book as "lessons" – and in the case of Holocaust history, "lessons of the Holocaust."

I began this book with a chapter on how historians nowadays are generally reluctant to adduce lessons about subjects they write about, whether they involve themes as varied as classical antiquity, the Protestant Reformation, the French Revolution, slavery, the First World War, or other events of equal importance. Holocaust history fits the pattern of such events. Most who write about the subject avoid the popular hunger for lessons of the Holocaust, even while our culture is replete with claims that these can be formulated. Coming from many different quarters, these lessons often contradict each other or distort history and warp our understanding. They are also crafted to serve a wide variety of present-day causes, and generally tell us more about the lesson definers than about events themselves. Moreover, there is something wrong when these lessons, even when unexceptionable propositions about human behaviour, unnecessarily invoke the Holocaust for their validation. And yet for all this I do believe that we learn a great deal from the history of the Holocaust. In this final chapter I explain how, even as historians of this subject have good reasons to eschew the pursuit of lessons as conventionally understood, their work not only deepens understanding of a great watershed in the history of our times but also enlarges our knowledge of the human condition.

Why do people study history? Most historians believe that their readers derive something more than entertainment from reading about the past – even as they do not all speak with one voice on what that something is, and even though they may not be fully clear in their own minds on that matter. Generally speaking, however, they seem to agree that a serious acquaintance with the past is intellectually enriching and facilitates our understanding of the world around us. Through the study of history, people acquire a deeper and more mature sense than they would otherwise of human capacities, how contexts interact with thought and action and institutions, how societies function and evolve, and how men and women engage with each other in public life. In other words, the study of history expands intellectual horizons, just as do other disciplines through their particular approaches to the human or natural worlds. In his memoirs, the veteran historian George Mosse once used the metaphor of travel when explaining his work, describing his aspirations to be "an intellectual not tied down to [his] starting point, solely guided by his analytical mind – something of an eternal traveler, analyzing, observing, suspended above events." History *is* like travel, only in time, even when not necessarily space; it takes us out of our present environment and to another, less familiar to us. It obliges us to became acquainted with a world that is not our own, and to do so systematically, guided by questions, not just random preconceptions or impressions. Of course, we eventually return from the voyage, but if we applied ourselves well to our trip we are the wiser for having left home; indeed, many would say, we are never quite the same as before we left.

How do we define those things that we pick up in our travels in time – and particularly travel to such horrifying places as the murder of European Jewry? I want to conclude this book with some thoughts about the kinds of things one *does* learn from Holocaust history. And I will do so, as I have with the preceding chapters, with reference to the area that I know best, namely my own involvement in this work as I have known it over the years.

Let us acknowledge that people do not approach Holocaust history with the equanimity of, say, early modern agriculture. People tell me that what I do is important, even urgent – although I usually feel embarrassed to hear them say that. Holocaust history remains alive in many people's memories and those of their families, even though there are fewer and fewer with direct experiences of its events. The human scars are evident if one looks closely – missing generations, psychological impacts transmitted to postwar collectivities, new generations, and new individuals. There are mental landscapes where the desolation is still quite evident, extending even to subsequent generations. History, moreover, provides no unified, consolatory view. As befits a vibrant field, there are lots of opinions about it, and an abundance of authorities. Survivors have special preoccupations, although these are less easily collapsed into a single prescription than is customarily assumed. Civic leaders may speak with one voice on commemorative and other occasions, but there are plenty of dissenters, and not all of them agree with each other. Some use Holocaust history for fundraising or political purposes; others are revolted by the prospect. Some Jewish leaders promote lessons of the Holocaust as a way of energizing Jewish identity, but others warn that it is unhealthy to define oneself as a perpetual victim, particularly when this defies current reality. Non-Jews are all over the map as well. Some have had enough. Some want to dig deeper. Other ethnic or national communities have special preoccupations and are concerned with how lessons of the Holocaust might reflect upon their own group. There are also different clusters of lessons on the Left and on the Right. Media offerings vary considerably, from the thoughtful and carefully articulated to the meretricious and clumsily worded.

I have wrestled with these issues for a long time. I remember, in the mid-1960s, debating with fellow graduate students, in Berkeley, about the larger context, namely the historian's craft. What was the historian's vocation? Opinions varied, but in my circle, in that heady Vietnam and civil rights era, most of us saw our task as social and political change. Politics lurked just beneath the surface of everything, we believed. (The title of my doctoral thesis and first book was *The Politics of Assimilation*.) We were to hold a mirror to society to show the seamy underside, and then to help set things right. There was plenty of presumption on our part. Our histories were sharply critical, and seldom celebratory. Lessons made sense in that environment, and young though we were, we did not shrink from pronouncing them.

I remember to this day the response to that view, which I now believe to have been the wiser course, and which was articulated by one of my instructors at the University of Toronto, universally respected as a master at his craft – even if not admired by us for his politics at the time. This was A.P. Thornton, as he was professionally known, a great student of the British Empire. A red-faced Scotsman who had been educated at the University of Glasgow and Trinity College, Oxford, "Archie," as I later knew him, was a veteran of the D-Day landings in France and had taught at Aberdeen and University College of the West Indies before coming to Toronto in the 1960s. To his Canadian students, he was the very embodiment of Empire. Later he was chairman of the department in Toronto, and I could imagine Archie answering the telephone, as did his counterpart in the film version of Kingsley Amis's comic academic novel, *Lucky Jim*, intoning, "History speaking." "The historian's job," Thornton insisted from his lectern – and I can remember his Scottish accent still, after more than sixty years – "is *to get it right!*" "Getting it right" was a sober and perhaps uninspiring injunction to youthful idealists because it suggested the diversion (as we saw it) of extraordinary energy into detail and tests of accuracy. But it also meant keeping an eye on the big picture. It meant the greatest care in research, wide-ranging reading, seeing documents in their original form, learning foreign languages, and studying the idioms of particular contexts. More often than not, it meant visits to dreary, ill-appointed archives (which, in truth, we loved), sifting paper for hours on end. Then as now, research required plenty of *Sitzfleisch*. This was a program sure to bring high-flying pronouncements down to earth, or discourage some from even getting off the ground. But it was the best advice we ever had.

"Getting it right" is what professional historians try to do and have a special obligation to do, in my view. According to convention, others may stray from this priority according to the dictates of occasion, conscience, public commitments, and fundamental beliefs. With Holocaust history, Jews and non-Jews, teachers and politicians, clergymen and artists, may all feel that they have professional reasons to treat the subject differently. I do not disparage such different approaches – far from it; at various moments, in other roles I perform, let us say on commemorative occasions, I may well engage the wartime murder of European Jews otherwise than as a professional historian. Some, however, have to make sure that the Holocaust upon which people act and ruminate is as faithful as one can get to the historical truth of the events themselves, or at least as faithful as we can possibly make it. Some have to be counted on for narrative accuracy, for explanatory generalizations that fit but do not exceed the evidence, and for a balanced view. Those are the historian's tasks, making him or her a custodian, in a sense, of the public memory of the event itself.

Just putting it this way, I know, makes some people uneasy, and quite often when I elaborate, they feel even worse. No one takes kindly to assertions of external authority in matters of the heart, and when memory has become sacralized, as has sometimes been the case with the murder of European Jewry, it can clash sharply with history as historians understand it. That is why academic lectures on Holocaust themes sometimes finish in stormy question and answer periods, with lecturers rushing for the exit at the end of the evening. "Let me tell you, it was not *quite* the way you have told us," questioners might say. Or, "Professor, that was a very nice lecture, but you *forgot* something." What then follows is another version of the subject at hand. "Getting it right" sometimes involves questioning the recollections of Holocaust survivors (although almost invariably there are other survivors who remember things differently), disputing received wisdom (although that wisdom has been received differently), pitting book learning against or at least alongside cherished or traumatic memories (although all of these may be contested by others in the audience). To younger colleagues contemplating this challenge, I can only say, *bon courage*!

There are significant compensations, however. I contend that the history of the Holocaust poses historical problems at least as challenging as, and often more challenging than, any other field I can imagine. "Getting it right" is extremely demanding; to do so investigators have available to them a vast documentation about perpetrators, victims, and bystanders – an availability that has significantly increased with the opening of archives in the former Soviet Union and Soviet-dominated countries. Those who do this work proceed by asking questions, and in the case of the Holocaust these are often of great moment. Some of these questions may fall outside the historian's province, for the answers may require a deeper understanding than we are capable of about humanity itself and its capacities for good and evil. But there are also myriad, garden-variety questions, asked and answered all the time by Holocaust historians, but in their case involving matters of sometimes extraordinary moral import: How were decisions about atrocities reached? How were they carried out? Who decided? Who acted? Who led? Who followed? Who helped? Who watched? Who knew? When? How? How did one place differ from another? Such questions, and many others, do not differ appreciably from those asked in other areas of inquiry – except that in the case of the Holocaust both the evidence and the answers involve issues of the gravest atrocities, murder, and other horrors, on a practically unimaginable scale.

"Getting it right" involves posing such questions and addressing them with the best tools the historical culture of our society provides. It entails putting ourselves in the shoes of others, often through the most vigorous efforts of the imagination, disciplined by the deepest and widest inquiry into the most varied of human circumstances. It also requires great efforts at objectivity, perhaps the most important methodological challenge for the student of the

Holocaust. Among the least appreciated and often contested attributes of the researcher these days, objectivity is nevertheless what we insist upon in many other aspects of life. There are many appropriate ways to respond to murder, but if we are speaking about an investigating officer, a coroner, or a judge, for example, we feel that their task requires them to keep an open mind about the evidence they assess and a capacity to weigh it fairly and dispassionately. When it comes to serious illness of someone close to us, we can respond appropriately, say, as friend, parent, or spouse, but we have quite different expectations when it comes to the surgeon conducting an operation. Indeed, with surgery, as with the practice of law or many other professional activities, we usually feel that too intimate a relationship might interfere with sound discharge of professional responsibilities. Simply put, we feel that practitioners such as these carry out their responsibilities best when they act as professionals.

No one expects, or desires, Holocaust specialists to perform like machines. But there is a world of difference between an inquiry as a sacred duty, keeping faith with those who were murdered – intimately involved with mourning, commemoration, denunciation, or a warning for future generations – and the quite different task of analysis, trying to deepen understanding in terms that are recognized by the general culture of our day. This last is the objective I am talking about here, an effort to integrate the history of the Holocaust into the general stream of historical consciousness, to apply to it the modes of analysis and the scholarly discourse used for other great issues of the day.

More than anything else, "getting it right" involves digesting this literature and asserting the place of the Holocaust in the wider history of our time. Disagreeing with Alvin Rosenfeld in his recent book, *The End of the Holocaust*, I do not accept that the Holocaust is shrinking from responsible historical memory and that those of us concerned with its place in history should lament its becoming "a volatile area of contending images, interpretations, historical claims and counter claims." I believe that Rosenfeld is right about the contestation – a matter about which we hear a great deal on the US Holocaust Memorial Museum's Academic Committee, which he chaired until recently. But I also believe that such disputation is evidence of the vigour of historical and other writing on the subject and its broad acceptance – one price of which is a degree of trivialization and vulgarization that seems to accompany any dominant public understanding, especially one that involves unprecedented human wrongdoing. Quite unlike the time of my youth, no one contemplating what has happened to mankind in the twentieth century can now avoid the Nazis' assault on European Jewry. Historians of the Third Reich now must all come to terms with it. Those who study the Second World War must do the same. Researchers from many different disciplinary backgrounds similarly cannot avoid the issue. Moralists and political theorists, sociologists and psychologists, religious thinkers and humanitarians must, at one point or another, consider the Holocaust. As Tony Judt once put it, "by the end of the twentieth century the centrality of the Holocaust in Western European identity and memory seemed secure." I would say the same for much of the rest of the industrialized world as well.

Most important, the effort to eliminate an entire people, set as a major objective by a highly developed industrial society and carried out on a European scale, is now widely seen to be unprecedented, not only for a European civilization but for humanity itself. The Holocaust is, as someone once put it, "the moral signifier of our age." In the past, peoples have constantly been cruel to one another, have tormented others in various ways, and have fantasized horribly about what might happen to their enemies. But there were always limits – imposed by politics, technology, humane sensibilities, religious scruples, geography, or military capacity. During the Second World War mankind crossed a terrible threshold. Nazi Germany operated without historic limits, until crushed by military force.

As a result, we have a different sense of human capacities than we did before. Some, particularly Jews who suffered at the hands of the Nazis but who miraculously survived, draw the bleakest conclusions of all. "Every day anew I lose my trust in the world," wrote Jean Améry, not long before his suicide. Others think that a warning is all one can deduce. Primo Levi's message was: "It can happen, and it can happen everywhere." Levi too ended his life, in all likelihood, but while he lived he argued that simply reflecting on the Holocaust might help prevent another catastrophe. Whatever one's view, the Holocaust has become a major reference point for our time, constantly kept in view for one's judgment about the state of the world – as once was the case, say, for the French Revolution or the First World War.

In addition to studying perpetrators, "getting it right" involves looking at victims, even while refusing to see them as endowed, by their victimization, with a special aura of heroism, righteousness, or other admirable qualities. When the Israeli research and commemorative institute Yad Vashem was founded in 1953, it was denoted in English as the Martyrs' and Heroes' Remembrance Authority. At the centre of attention, in the words of the law establishing the institution, was a distinctly Israeli appreciation of the victims' experiences – "the sublime, persistent struggle of the masses of the House of Israel, on the threshold of destruction, for their human dignity and Jewish culture." The accent was on combativeness, rebellion, and unwillingness to submit. The principal outcome was national regeneration through resistance and armed struggle. No sooner had Yad Vashem been established, however, than a different Israeli voice was heard. In 1954 the Hebrew poet Natan Alterman, who has been called "the uncrowned poet laureate" of his Israeli generation and who lived in Palestine during the war, wrote a famous poem celebrating Jewish *opponents* of the insurgents – those who claimed "resistance will destroy us all." A dissident voice at the time, Alterman took care to appreciate as the real heroes those Jews who were caught in the middle – heads of the Jewish Councils or *Judenräte*, confused and harassed community leaders, those responsible elders who "negotiated and complied," rather than the relatively small number of young people who managed to take up arms. Following Alterman's intervention, an intense debate began, which has renewed itself with new discoveries and new historical writing, and it has continued ever since – most recently in a book on ghetto leaders by my Israeli colleague Dan Michman, *The Emergence of Jewish Ghettos during the Holocaust*. In this way, Holocaust history regenerates. The result, I believe, has been a greater historical understanding, enriched by research and the confrontation of different points of view.

Finally, "getting it right" involves finding the right language, expressing oneself in the right idiom – speaking with a voice, in short, appropriate both for the most terrible events and also for the most recent generation to take up this field. Holocaust history is like all history in this respect; it must constantly be rewritten if it is not to vanish from public perceptions or lose the significance we want ascribed to it. Here again, Holocaust history poses special challenges. In his *Reflections of Nazism*, published over thirty years ago, Saul Friedländer dwelt upon the difficulties historians and others have in finding the right words to discuss the massacre of European Jewry. Friedländer worried about what he felt was an unhealthy fascination with Nazism, evident particularly in films and literature. This is part of the problem of how we communicate things that are deeply disturbing, but also strange to us and difficult to grasp emotionally – and it is of course a problem that is with us still. Historians neutralize horror, Friedländer seems to say; and he was concerned with expression that "normalizes, smoothes and neutralizes our vision of the past." Does scholarly discourse anaesthetize in this way? Friedländer knew that there is no easy answer. "There should be no misunderstanding about what I am trying to say: The historian cannot work in any other way, and historical studies have to be pursued along the accepted lines. The events described are what is unusual, not the historians' work. We have reached the limit of our means of expression."

There is no alternative, I conclude, but to keep at it. Students of the Holocaust are called upon to provide various kinds of explanation, and their preoccupation is not only the intractable material they work with, but also a public that is constantly coming forward with new layers of experience, new interests, and new unfamiliarity. Diaries and memoirs of survivors reflect a widely shared obsession of those who lived and died in the Holocaust: "How will what happened to us be understood?" "Could a postwar world possibly grasp what we went through?" Imagine how those victims might understand the generation that now looks back on their agonies. The gap grows wider, and with it the challenge to historians and everyone else.

For all of those concerned to see knowledge about the Holocaust extended so that such things might be prevented in the future, I think we have something that is more durable than lessons, which in any event were bound to evolve and change with the passage of time. The Holocaust has become history, has entered into the historical canon, with all of its strengths and weaknesses. This means disputation and disagreement, but also research, new questions, and new ways of looking at old problems. It means writers and researchers around the world, and with many different backgrounds, applying themselves to the task of understanding, which is predicated upon the requirement to "get it right." This is the way, in our culture, that historical understanding is preserved and advanced. It seems plain now that, after the shock of the postwar era, the Holocaust has become history. That is certainly the best guarantee we have that it will be remembered. As to the future, the preserve of lessons, no one knows whether a deeper understanding such as I am promoting here can enable societies to avoid the catastrophes of the past. All I can suggest is that we are better equipped to do so than if we abandoned such an effort. Studying the Holocaust deepens appreciation of human reality, and that, in a general sense, makes us more mature, wiser, more "experienced" observers of the human scene.

Acknowledgments

Part memoir, part analysis, part historiography, this book is the product of much rumination over years of study, research, teaching, and lecturing on the history of the Holocaust – at the University of Toronto, the University of California at Berkeley, St Antony's College, Oxford, UCLA, the University of Cape Town, and numerous other venues in Canada, the United States, Europe, and Israel. I feel honoured to have had the opportunity to appear at some very distinguished institutions, to have been so warmly received, and to have engaged with students, colleagues, and members of the general public who have had the patience to hear me out over the years. I am especially grateful to my home institution, the University of Toronto, where I first found my way in intellectual matters more than a half a century ago, and where I have taught for more than forty-five years – including some as the Chancellor Rose and Ray Wolfe Professor of Holocaust Studies. Within that home, I have been particularly fortunate to be a part of the wonderful community of colleagues and students at Massey College, led over the past nineteen years by the exemplary Master John Fraser, and now his successor, the Honourable Hugh Segal. These fine institutions have provided me with the space, libraries, time, collegiality, feedback, and above all encouragement to pursue work that I enjoyed – and to do so freely, without intellectual hindrance of any kind. What more could one expect from these places of learning? The least I can do is to offer my heartfelt appreciation.

Focusing on "lessons of the Holocaust," this book is a way of explaining to myself and others what I have been doing at the various institutions I have mentioned. This has not always been easy to clarify. I have spent much time attempting to do so in conversations with my successor as Wolfe Professor, Doris Bergen, exchanging views about our varied responsibilities in teaching Holocaust history, why we frankly enjoy working in this exceptionally grim subject of study, and what we think is the point of it all. I am extraordinarily appreciative of the way in which her vigour and intelligence have helped me maintain my own enthusiasm for my field, not to mention my continuing understanding of it. I want also to record the debt I owe to wonderful mentors, teachers, colleagues, friends, and students in history and other disciplines, people with whom it has been a privilege and pleasure to work and learn from over the years – and this when in agreement or disagreement, sometimes on matters that touch upon the very nature of the Holocaust itself. Some of these appear by name in the pages of this book, but this is the place to thank them all. I want to add that I particularly appreciate how this engagement continues now that I have formally retired, representing a never-ending quest to get to the bottom of things. I have chosen lessons as my unifying theme because I sense that this is how many people understand the work of Holocaust historians. Certainly "lessons" is the most popular designation of what the Holocaust is supposed to teach. My own view is that this is a misperception, and I believe that the best way I can explain what I do is to discuss just why I think this way. That is the subject of this book.

Meanwhile, and taking of course sole responsibility for what I have written here, I want to thank all of those who have assisted me by discussing these issues either in a general or very specific way, and in some cases even taking the trouble to review an earlier draft of this book. These include Howard Adelman, Steven Aschheim, Doris Bergen, Leora Bilsky, Michael Bliss, Rivka Brot, Christopher Browning, Roger Errera, Eugene Fisher, Louis Greenspan, Peter Hayes, Shira Herzog, Susannah Heschel, Gerald Izenberg, Naomi Kriss, Tamar Liebes, Wendy Lower, Dow Marmur, Michael

Morgan, Robert Paxton, Derek Penslar, Anna Porter, Brenda Proulx, Seymour Reich, Milton Shain, Janice Stein, and Bernard Wasserstein. In a special category of thanks for her advice is my literary agent, Beverley Slopen, from whom I have learned, over the years, to listen carefully even when it is painful, and to revisit a manuscript even when I want to send it off. And finally, I want to record that, happily for me, all of these opinions can be set against those of my wife, Carol Randi Marrus, who has never let me sink too low or to rise too high, both with what is here and what is not. This book is dedicated to her.

Massey College in the University of Toronto
June 2015

Principal Sources

Chapter 1. Public and Personal Lessons

Joan Shelley Rubin, *The Making of Middlebrow Culture*; Arno Mayer, *Why Did the Heavens Not Darken*; Walter Laqueur, *Best of Times, Worst of Times*; Margaret MacMillan, *Dangerous Games: The Uses and Abuses of History*; Alon Confino, *Foundational Pasts: The Holocaust as Historical Understanding*; Robert Bothwell, *Laying the Foundation*; George L. Mosse, *Confronting History*; Jonathan Webber, *The Future of Auschwitz: Some Personal Reflections*.

Chapter 2. Historical Lessons

J.G.A. Pocock, "Historiography and Enlightenment: A View of Their Study," *Modern Intellectual History* 5 (2008); Michael Horowitz and Cynthia Palmer, eds., *Moksha: Aldous Huxley's Writings on Psychedelics and the Visionary Experience (1931–1963)*; Pierre Nora, "Between Memory and History: *Les Lieux de Mémoire*," *Representations* 26 (1989); Henry Rousso, *The Haunting Past: History, Memory, and Justice in Contemporary France*; Daniel Schacter, *The Seven Sins of Memory: How the Mind Forgets and Remembers*; Tony Judt, *Postwar: A History of Europe since 1945*; Murray G. Murphey, *Our Knowledge of the Historical Past*; Arthur Schlesinger, Jr, review of Ernest R. May, "The Use and Misuse of History in American Foreign Policy," *Journal of American History* 61 (1974); Otto Friedrich, *Before the Deluge: A Portrait of Berlin in the 1920s*; Geoffrey Elton, *Return to Essentials: Some Reflections on the Present State of Historical Study*; idem, *The Practice of History*; Jacques Ellul, *The Technological Society*; Margaret MacMillan, *Dangerous Games: The Uses and Abuses of History*; William Bain, "Are There Any Lessons of History? The English School and the Activity of Being an Historian," *International Politics*

44 (2007); Yuen Foong Khong, *Analogies at War: Korea, Munich, Dien Bien Phu, and the Vietnam Decisions of 1965*; Bernard Lonergan, *Method in Theology*; Charlotte Smith, *Carl Becker on History and the Climate of Opinion*; Barbara Tuchman, "History Lessons," *New York Review of Books*, March 29, 1984; Paul Johnson, "Tuchman's Folly," *New Criterion*, May 1984; Harold Evans, "On the Brink," *New York Times Book Review*, May 19, 2013; Ernest May, *"Lessons" of the Past: The Use and Misuse of History in American Foreign Policy*; Kathleen Burk, *Troublemaker: The Life and History of A.J.P. Taylor*; Michael Howard, *The Lessons of History*; "Liberté pour l'histoire," *Libération*, December 13, 2005; Pierre Nora, "History, Memory and the Law in France, 1990–2010," *Historein* 11 (2011); Millennium Project, *Global Futures Studies and Research*.

Chapter 3. Early Lessons

Telford Taylor, *The Anatomy of the Nuremberg Trials*; Myriam Anissimov, *Primo Levi: Tragedy of an Optimist*; Ian Thomson, *Primo Levi: A Life*; Naomi Seidman, "Elie Wiesel and the Scandal of Jewish Rage," *Jewish Social Studies* 3 (1996); Naomi Seidman, *Faithful Renderings: Jewish-Christian Differences and the Politics of Translation*; Susan Rubin Suleiman, "Problems of Memory and Factuality in Recent Holocaust Memoirs: Wilkomerski/Wiesel," *Poetics Today* 21 (2000); Raul Hilberg, *The Politics of Memory: The Journey of a Holocaust Historian*; Alon Confino, "Remembering the Second World War, 1945–1965: Narratives of Victimhood and Genocide," *Cultural Analysis* 4 (2005); Tony Judt, *Postwar: A History of Europe since 1945*; Annette Wieviorka, *The Era of the Witness*; Christopher R. Browning, Susannah Heschel, Michael R. Marrus, and Milton Shain, eds., *Holocaust Scholarship: Personal Trajectories and Professional Interpretations*; Hasia Diner, *We Remember with Reverence and Love*; Tony Judt, "The 'Problem of Evil' in Postwar Europe," *New York Review of Books*, February 14, 2008; Idith Zertal, *Israel's Holocaust and the Politics of Nationhood*; Claude Lanzmann, *The Patagonian Hare: A Memoir*; Sharon Portnoff, James A. Diamond, and Martiln D. Yaffe, eds., *Emil L. Fackenheim: Philosopher, Theologian, Jew*; Michael L. Morgan, *Fackenheim's Jewish Philosophy: An Introduction*; Peter Novick, *The Holocaust in American Life*; Alvin Rosenfeld, *Thinking about the Holocaust after Half a Century*; Gregory Baum, *Essays in Critical Philosophy*; Edward T. Linenthal, *Preserving Memory: The Struggle to Create America's Holocaust Museum*; Jonathan Tobin, "Six Million Dead but Eleven, or Is It Twelve Million Universalizing Lies," *Commentary*, December 2014; Tom Segev, *Simon Wiesenthal: The Life and Legend*; Sam Shulman, "Holocaust Hegemony ... and Its Moral Pitfalls," *Weekly Standard*, January 3, 2011.

Chapter 4. Jewish Lessons

Raul Hilberg, *The Politics of Memory: The Journey of a Holocaust Historian*; Christopher R. Browning; *Nazi Policy, Jewish Workers, German Killers*; Lawrence Langer, *Pre-empting the Holocaust*; Jean Améry, *At the Mind's Limits: Contemplations by a Survivor on Auschwitz and Its Realities*; Elie Wiesel, *Night*; Elie Pfefferkorn, *The Muselmann at the Water Cooler*; Annette Wieviorka, *The Era of the Witness*; Barbara Engelking, *Holocaust and Memory: The Experience of the Holocaust and Its Consequences: An Investigation Based on Personal Narratives*; Christopher R. Browning, *Remembering Survival: Inside a Nazi Slave-Labor Camp*; Doris Bergen, *War and Genocide: A Concise History of the Holocaust*; Amos Goldberg, *Holocaust Diaries as "Life Stories"*; Margaret MacMillan, *Dangerous Games: The Uses and Abuses of History*; Elisabeth Young-Bruehl, *Hannah Arendt: For the Love of the World*; Etgar Keret, *The Seven Good Years: A Memoir*; Ruth R. Wisse, *Jews and Power*; Klaus-Michael Mallmann and Martin Cüppers, *Nazi Palestine: The Plans for the Extermination of the Jews in Palestine*; Richard Bretiman and Allan J. Lichtman, *FDR and the Jews*; Michael R. Marrus, "FDR and the Holocaust: From Blaming to Understanding," *Yad Vashem Studies*; Raphael Ahren, "The Holocaust Can Happen Again, Warns Top Anti-Semitism Scholar," *Haaretz*, April 12, 2010; Edward Alexander, *The State of the Jews: A Critical Appraisal*; Alvin H. Rosenfeld, *Anne Frank and the Future of Holocaust Memory*; Daniel Greenfield, "Israel, the Holocaust and the Survival Lesson," *Outpost*, April 2010; Peter Hirschberg, "Netanyahu: It's 1938 and Iran Is Germany: Ahmadinejad Is Preparing Another Holocaust," *Haaretz*, November 14, 2006; Nicole Herrington, "Viewing Anti-Semitism from a Global Angle," *New York Times*, October 18, 2012; Phyllis Chesler, "Can the Brainwashed Learn the Lessons of the Holocaust in Time?" *News Real Blog*, October 4, 2010, http://www.newsrealblog.com/2010/10/04/can-the-brainwashed-learn-the-lessons-of-the-holocaust-in-time/, consulted on December 10, 2014; Fareed Zakaria, "The Year of Living Fearfully," *Newsweek*, September 11, 2006.

Chapter 5. Israeli Lessons

Bernard Avishai Dot com, May 14, 2009. http://bernardavishai.blogspot.ca/2009/05/pope-and-rubys-tuesday.html; Boaz Cohen, "Setting the Agenda of Holocaust Research: Discord at Yad Vashem in the 1950s," in David Bankier and Dan Michman, eds., *Holocaust Historiography in Context: Emergence, Challenges, Polemics and Achievements*; Ronald Zweig, *German Reparations and the Jewish World: A History of the Claims Conference*; Anna

Porter, *Kasztner's Train: The True Story of Rezso Kasztner, Unknown Hero of the Holocaust*; Leora Bilsky, *Transformative Justice: Israeli Identity on Trial*; Tom Segev, *The Seventh Million: The Israelis and the Holocaust*; Hanna Yablonka, *The State of Israel vs. Adolf Eichmann*; Bettina Stangneth, *Eichmann before Jerusalem: The Unexamined Life of a Mass Murderer*; Idith Zertal, *Israel's Holocaust and the Politics of Nationhood*; Yehiam Weitz, "Ben Gurion and the Eichmann Trial," *Yad Vashem Studies* 36 (2008); "The Eichmann Case As Seen by Ben Gurion," *New York Times Magazine*, January 8, 1961; Ronald W. Zweig, *David Ben-Gurion: Politics and Leadership in Israel*; Nahum Goldmann, *The Autobiography of Nahum Goldmann: Sixty Years of Jewish Life*; Lawrence Douglas, *The Memory of Judgment: Making Law and History in the Trials of the Holocaust*; Annette Wieviorka, *The Era of the Witness*; Amit Pinchevsky and Tamar Liebes, "Severed Voices: Radio and the Mediation of Trauma in the Eichmann Trial," *Public Culture* 22 (2010); David Cesarani, *Becoming Eichmann: Rethinking the Life, Crimes, and Trial of a "Desk Murderer"*; Michal Shaked, "The Unknown Eichmann Trial: The Story of the Judge," *Holocaust and Genocide Studies* 29 (2015); Daniel Levy and Natan Sznaider, *The Holocaust and Memory in the Global Age*; Avraham Burg, *The Holocaust Is Over: We Must Rise from Its Ashes*; Steven Aschheim, in Christopher Browning, Susannah Heschel, Michael Marrus, and Milton Shain, eds., *Holocaust Scholarship: Personal Trajectories and Professional Interpretations*; Merav Michaeli, "Israel's Never-Ending Holocaust," *Haaretz*, January 20, 2012; Eyal Lewin, *Ethos Clash in Israeli Society*; Ruthie Blum, "Recalling the Nazi Parallel," *Jerusalem Post*, April 27, 2014; Galia Golan, *Israeli Peacemaking since 1967: Factors behind the Breakthroughs and Failures*; Yossi Klein Halevi, "Resolving Israel's Internal War of Atonement," *Times of Israel*, September 9, 2013; Meir Kahane, *Never Again: A Program for Survival*; Avi Shilon, *Menachem Begin: A Life*; Aluf Benn, "The Short History of the Future Holocaust," *Haaretz*, June 3, 2013; Amira Hass, "Life under Israeli Occupation – by an Israeli," *Independent*, August 26, 2001; Allan C. Brownfield, "The Politicization of the Holocaust: Examining the Uses and Abuse of Its Legacy," *Washington Report on Middle East Affairs*, October/November 1998; "Full Transcript of Netanyahu Speech for Remembrance Day," *Times of Israel*, April 27, 2014; Herb Keinon, Nissan Tsur, "PM: Israel Ready to Defend against Another Holocaust," *Jerusalem Post*, June 13, 2013; Benjamin Gampel, "Benzion Netanyahu, Scholar Who Saw Lessons in History: Appreciation," *Jewish Daily Forward*, May 2, 2012; David Remnick, "The Outsider," *New Yorker*, May 25, 1998; Arye Naor, "Lessons of the Holocaust versus Territories for Peace, 1967–2001," *Israel Studies* 8 (2003); Jeffrey Goldberg, "The Point of No Return," *Atlantic*, August 11, 2010; Yehuda Bauer, "The Israel Air Force Flyover at Auschwitz: A Crass, Superficial

Display," *Haaretz*, October 8, 2013; Tony Judt, "The Problem of Evil in Postwar Europe," *New York Review of Books*, February 14, 2008.

Chapter 6. Universal Lessons

Hannah Arendt, *Eichmann in Jerusalem: A Report on the Banality of Evil*; Gertrude Erzorsky, "Hannah Arendt against the Facts," *New Politics* 2 (1963); Susan Neiman, "Theodicy in Jerusalem," in Steven E. Aschheim, ed., *Hannah Arendt in Jerusalem*; "Polish Philosopher Bauman Rejects Honorary Degree over Anti-Semitic Attacks," *JTA*, August 19, 2013; Michael Berenbaum, *The Vision of the Void: Theological Reflections on the Works of Eli Wiesel*; idem, "What the Survivor and the Historian Know," *Jewish Daily Forward*, May 4, 2012; Marion Fischel, "The 50 Most Influential Jews of 2014," *Jerusalem Post*, June 3, 2014; Elie Wiesel, *One Generation After*; Michael Ignatieff, *The Warrior's Honour: Ethnic War and the Modern Conscience*; Alan S. Rosenbaum, *Is the Holocaust Unique? Perspectives on Comparative Genocide*; Emil Fackenheim, *A Jewish Philosopher's Response to the Holocaust*; Michael R. Marrus, *Some Measure of Justice: The Holocaust Era Restitution Campaign of the 1990s*; Jan Surmann, "Restitution Policy and the Transformation of Holocaust Memory: The Impact of the American 'Crusade for Justice' after 1989," *Bulletin of the German Historical Institute* 49 (Fall 2011); Irwin Cotler, "An Act of Remembrance, a Remembrance to Act," *Jerusalem Post*, February 1, 2011; Daniel Jonah Goldhagen, *Hitler's Willing Executioners: Ordinary Germans and the Holocaust*; Daniel Mendelsohn, *The Lost: A Search for Six of the Six Million*; Doris L. Bergen, "Studying the Holocaust: Is History Commemoration?" in Dan Stone, ed., *The Holocaust and Historical Methodology*; Peter Hayes, "The Holocaust: Myths and Misconceptions," unpub. paper.

Chapter 7. Lessons of the Holocaust

Stanley Payne, David Sorkin, and John Tortorice, *What History Tells: George L. Mosse and the Culture of Modern Europe*; George L. Mosse, *Confronting History: A Memoir*; Alvin Rosenfeld, *The End of the Holocaust*; Tony Judt, "From the House of the Dean: On Modern European Memory," *New York Review of Books*, October 6, 2005; Leora Bilsky, "In a Different Voice: Nathan Alterman and Hannah Arendt on the Kastner and Eichmann Trials," *Theoretical Inquires in Law* 1 (2000).

Index